Working One-to-One with Students

Working One-to-One with Students is written for higher education academics, adjuncts, teaching assistants and research students who are looking for guidance inside and outside the classroom. This book is a jargon-free, practical guide to improving one-to-one teaching, covering a wide range of teaching contexts, including mentoring students and staff, supervising dissertations and how to approach informal meetings outside of lectures.

Written in an engaging, accessible style and grounded in experience, this book offers a combination of practical advice backed by relevant learning theory. Featuring a wealth of case studies and useful resources, the book covers areas including:

■ supporting students
■ encouraging independent learning
■ mentoring coaching and personal tutoring
■ developing peer groups and buddying programmes
■ dealing with diversity, difficult students and ethical dilemmas
■ supervising the undergraduate dissertation
■ supervising postgraduates in the Arts, Social Sciences and Sciences.

This book is a short, snappy, practical guide that covers this key element of a lecturer's work. In the spirit of the series (*Key Guides for Effective Teaching in Higher Education*) this book covers relevant theory that effectively informs practice.

Gina Wisker is Head of Learning and Teaching, Centre for Learning and Teaching, University of Brighton.
Kate Exley is an Education Consultant and Series Editor of the *Key Guides for Effective Teaching in Higher Education* series.
Maria Antoniou is Research Fellow at the Centre for Learning and Teaching, University of Brighton.
Pauline Ridley is a Senior Lecturer at the Centre for Learning and Teaching, University of Brighton.

APR 10

CH

Key Guides for Effective Teaching in Higher Education Series
Edited by Kate Exley

This indispensable series is aimed at new lecturers, postgraduate students who have teaching time, Graduate Teaching Assistants, part-time tutors and demonstrators, as well as experienced teaching staff who may feel it's time to review their skills in teaching and learning.

Titles in this series will provide the teacher in higher education with practical, realistic guidance on the various different aspects of their teaching role, which is underpinned not only by current research in the field, but also by the extensive experience of individual authors, and with a keen eye kept on the limitations and opportunities therein. By bridging a gap between academic theory and practice, all titles will provide generic guidance on teaching, learning and assessment issues, which is then brought to life through the use of short illustrative examples drawn from a range of disciplines. All titles in the series will:

■ represent up-to-date thinking and incorporate the use of computing and information technology (C&IT) where appropriate
■ consider methods and approaches for teaching and learning when there is an increasing diversity in learning and a growth in student numbers
■ encourage reflexive practice and self-evaluation, and a means of developing the skills of teaching, learning and assessment
■ provide links and references to other work on the topic and research evidence where appropriate.

Titles in the series will prove invaluable whether they are used for self-study or as part of a formal induction programme on teaching in higher education (HE), and will also be of relevance to teaching staff working in further education (FE) settings.

Other titles in this series:

Assessing Skills and Practice
  – Sally Brown and Ruth Pickford
Assessing Students' Written Work: Marking Essays and Reports
  – Catherine Haines
Designing Learning: From Module Outline to Effective Teaching
  – Chris Butcher, Clara Davies and Melissa Highton
Developing Your Teaching: Ideas, Insight and Action
  – Peter Kahn and Lorraine Walsh
Enhancing Learning Through Formative Assessment and Feedback
  – Alastair Irons
Giving a Lecture: From Presenting to Teaching
  – Kate Exley and Reg Dennick
Small Group Teaching
  – Kate Exley and Reg Dennick
Using C&IT to Support Teaching
  – Paul Chin

Working One-to-One with Students

Supervising, Coaching, Mentoring, and Personal Tutoring

Gina Wisker
Kate Exley
Maria Antoniou
Pauline Ridley

Routledge
Taylor & Francis Group

NEW YORK AND LONDON

First published 2008
by Routledge
270 Madison Ave, New York, NY 10016

Simultaneously published in the UK
by Routledge
2 Park Square, Milton Park, Abingdon, Oxon OX14 4RN

Routledge is an imprint of the Taylor & Francis Group, an informa business

© 2008 Routledge, Taylor and Francis

Typeset in Perpetua by
Florence Production Ltd, Stoodleigh, Devon
Printed and bound in the United States of America
on acid-free paper by
Edwards Brothers, Inc.

Library of Congress Cataloging in Publication Data
    Working one-to-one with students: supervising, coaching,
    mentoring, and personal tutoring/Gina Wisker . . . [*et al.*].
        p. cm.
    Includes bibliographical references.
        1. Individualized instruction—Great Britain.   2. College
teaching—Great Britain.   I. Wisker, Gina, 1951–
LB1031.W65 2008
371.39′4—dc22   2007051020

ISBN10: 0–415–36530–9 (hbk)
ISBN10: 0–415–36531–7 (pbk)
ISBN10: 0–203–01649–1 (ebk)

ISBN13: 978–0–415–36530–7 (hbk)
ISBN13: 978–0–415–36531–4 (pbk)
ISBN13: 978–0–203–01649–7 (ebk)

Contents

CONTENTS

Series preface

THE SERIES

The *Key Guides for Effective Teaching in Higher Education* were initially discussed as an idea in 2002 and the first group of four titles was published in 2004. New titles have continued to be added and the series now boasts nine books (with more in the pipeline).

The series includes:

- *Giving a Lecture: from presenting to teaching*, Exley and Dennick (2004)
- *Small Group Teaching: seminars, tutorials and beyond*, Exley and Dennick (2004)
- *Assessing Students' Written Work: marking essays and reports*, Haines (2004)
- *Using C&IT to Support Teaching*, Chin (2004)
- *Designing Learning: from module outline to effective teaching*, Butcher, Davies and Highton (2006)
- *Assessing Skills and Practice*, Brown and Pickford (2006)
- *Developing Your Teaching: ideas, insight and action*, Kahn and Walsh (2006)
- *Enhancing Learning Through Formative Assessment and Feedback*, Irons (2007)
- and this volume, *Working One-to-One with Students: supervising, coaching, mentoring and personal tutoring*, Wisker, Exley, Antoniou and Ridley (2008).

The tenth volume, *Inclusivity and Diversity* by Sue Grace and Phil Gravestock, together with a new and updated, second edition of the popular *Giving a Lecture* title should be with you shortly.

It has always been intended that the books would be primarily of use to new teachers in universities and colleges. It has been exciting to see them being used to support Postgraduate Certificate programmes in teaching and learning for new academic staff and clinical teachers and also the skills training programmes for postgraduate students and Graduate Teaching Assistants (GTAs) who are beginning to teach. A less anticipated, but very valued, readership has been the experienced teachers who have dipped into the books when reviewing their teaching and have given the authors feedback and made further suggestions on teaching approaches and examples of practice.

THIS BOOK

I am delighted that *Working One-to-One with Students* now joins the series. I know it has been eagerly awaited by some who spend much of their 'teaching time' supervising undergraduate and postgraduate project and dissertation students. However, I believe this book is unique in its scope. It seeks to address a wider range of one-to-one learning situations and considers the skills, knowledge and teaching techniques important in each. The book includes chapters on the complex role of the academic/personal tutor (PT), which may involve providing both study guidance and pastoral support – a demanding role, particularly if tutees have personal problems or disability and mental health concerns. The support of students on placements, at a distance and online is considered, along with the one-to-one coaching more experienced teachers can provide for their newer colleagues. I do feel that the book fits snugly in the 'fold' as the themes that shaped the series are clearly felt and visible throughout its pages.

KEY THEMES OF THE SERIES

The books are all attempting to combine two things – to be very practical and to provide lots of examples of methods and techniques and also to link to educational theory and underpinning research. Articles are referenced, further readings are suggested and researchers in the field are quoted.

There is also much enthusiasm here to link to the wide range of teaching development activities thriving in the disciplines, supported by the excellent work of national teaching bodies such as the Higher Education Academy Subject Centres and the Centres for Excellence in Teaching and

Learning (CETLs) in the UK. Indeed, both the Subject Centres and the CETLS are frequently recommended as further sources of information and suggested as useful points of contact, throughout the volumes. The need to tailor teaching approaches to meet the demands of different subject areas and to provide new teachers with examples of practice that are easily recognisable in their fields of study, is seen as being very important by all the authors. To this end, the books include many examples drawn from a wide range of academic subjects and different kinds of higher education institutions.

This theme of diversity is also embraced when considering the heterogeneous groups of students we now teach. Student cohorts include people of different ages, experience, ability, culture, language, etc., and all the books include discussion of the issues and demands this places on teachers in today's universities. Where appropriate this might include guidance on current legislation and shared views on good practice in teaching for inclusivity.

In the books of the series there is also more than half an eye trying to peer into the future – what will lectures look like in ten or twenty years time? How will we assess and tutor our students? How will student expectations, government policy, funding streams, and new technological advances and legislation affect what happens in our learning spaces of the future? You will see, therefore, that many of the books do include chapters that aim to look ahead and tap into the thinking of our most innovative and creative teachers in an attempt to crystal ball gaze.

So, these were the original ideas underpinning the series and I and my co-authors have tried hard to keep them in mind as we researched our topics and typed away. We really hope that you find the books to be useful and interesting, whether you are a new teacher, just starting out in your teaching career, or you are an experienced teacher reflecting on your practice and reviewing what you do.

Kate Exley
Series Editor

Acknowledgements

This book is an example of networking and sharing across institutions. It began when the main author and editor, Gina Wisker, was at Anglia Ruskin, and planned it with Dr Kate Exley from the University of Leeds, but has been written while Gina has settled into the University of Brighton, with co-authors Dr Maria Antoniou and Pauline Ridley, from Brighton, Kate Exley, and support and contributions from Charlotte Morris, who moved from Anglia to Brighton during the process. Throughout, Charlotte Morris and Michelle Bernard have supported its production and, latterly, the Brighton team of Emily Thompson, Zoe Murrin and Lana Burgess have helped finalise it, with Michelle's meticulous eye for detail. We are very grateful to Routledge for their patience with the complexities of settling into new jobs, which hindered but enriched its completion.

Thanks to Palgrave Macmillan for some quotations from Gina's *The Good Supervisor* (2005) and *The Postgraduate Research Handbook* (2001, 2nd edn, 2007) and the University of Brighton for re-use of internal documents on personal tutoring.

We would all like to thank our long suffering families and colleagues for tolerance and support during the development and production of the book.

Introduction

Supervising, mentoring, coaching and personal tutoring: working one-to-one with students

Students remember and really value working one-to-one with teachers and tutors in a variety of roles, recognising the importance of a focus on their learning as an individual. There is a wealth of literature on lecturing, on developing small group teaching and the essential nature of developing student autonomy and independent learners. Working one-to-one is just one of the ways in which we support and empower students in their learning and it is not the intention of this book to suggest it is the only, or the best way, rather that it is one we need to retain as an important part of the jigsaw of learning and teaching opportunities. Teaching students on an individual basis and supporting their learning face-to-face, one-to-one, seems in many ways to have become a dim and cherished memory as student numbers increase, modular systems lead to large, faceless masses in lecture theatres, and students themselves find they are rarely in a group with the same other students twice in a week. However, it is precisely because of this increase in numbers and relative fragmentation that the kind of personalised support we might remember having ourselves as undergraduates needs to be reinvented in a variety of contemporary, imaginative, flexible and diverse shapes to suit the needs of today's mass higher education (HE), and the diversity of students.

This book is co-written by three members of the Centre of Learning and Teaching at Brighton, and a learning and teaching consultant from the University of Leeds, with some references and inputs from others at Brighton and elsewhere. It draws on a wealth of experience in working as personal tutors, coaching, mentoring, supervising, working with the individual needs of students in study skills and Ph.D. supervising sessions, nurturing early days of personal development planning (PDP) and similar strategies to engage students as learners owning their own learning development. It draws on experience of working with international students at a distance, developing buddy systems to support the one-to-one work with group-oriented sessions, and working with students from a variety of learning backgrounds, from mature to younger in age. At least one of us has had the experience of tutoring in the Oxbridge system and the pleasures and perils of that intense interaction, recently researched by Graham Gibbs and Keith Trigwell. At least one of us has worked in teaching as a private tutor, recognising the vast range of needs and abilities close-up as you work with the specific learning needs of an individual and match your work rhythms to theirs. Most of us have in some way been mentored, coached, have experienced the personal tutoring system and have been supervised through an individual, longer, research-oriented or work-related piece of work, report, dissertation or Ph.D. thesis. We have all worked with a vast range of students and, so, with a variety of learning approaches and of disabilities and mental health issues. We have combined across our various experiences and expertise on the receiving and delivering/engaging end of one-to-one teaching and learning and have drawn on that of colleagues and discussion lists to make what we intend to be useful suggestions in a contemporary context for HE staff, and those staff in further education colleges who teach on HE courses and who are keen to undertake the effective and essential kind of work that today's students need, and which ultimately enables them to become autonomous learners who own and can direct their own learning, beable to work independently, to link in groups with others locally and at a distance, and able to articulate to employers their achieved skills.

CHANGING EXPECTATIONS

Recent changes in UK HE have led to the need for a diversity of forms of learning and teaching. The government's White Paper 'The Future of Higher Education' (DfES, 2003a), and the subsequent 'Widening Parti-cipation' document (DfES, 2003b) set out a vision for an expanded and more inclusive HE sector. The government aims that 50 per cent of the UK's 18–30 year olds should have experience of studying within HE. To achieve this, university funding is now tied to the development of strategies for improving access to, and support within, HE for 'socially disadvantaged' individuals and groups. Even in the context of increased fees and top-up fees, traditional aged and mature students are entering HE in large numbers, some of them with conventional qualifications and others with work and/or domestic experience, and experience from access or foundation courses, where there might well be issues of different learning expectations when they transition into full-time HE. There are increasing numbers of international students for whom English is not their first language or mother tongue, and the biggest growth area is actually among postgraduates who represent all kinds of learning styles approaches, origins and discipline areas and, depending on the discipline of postgraduate students, will be required to work autonomously, and in many cases to work almost entirely independently, but supported and guided in this by their supervisor.

The increased number of students in HE (sometimes termed 'massi-fication'), and the greater diversity of students' backgrounds, experiences and abilities, means that traditional methods of learning and teaching might no longer work. HE is seeing a shift from directive means of teaching such as lecturing, to methods that encourage students to work independently and in small groups to achieve their learning aims. Distance-learning is a current growth area in UK HE, with universities reaching large numbers of both UK-based and international students off-campus through new technologies such as video conferencing and blogging ('web log' or diary) facilities.

Today's students typically have less contact time with HE teachers than they previously enjoyed. The HE teacher not only has responsi-bility for a greater number of students, but must also juggle competing pressures to teach, research and publish, undertake administration and also, increasingly, to become involved in community and local business initiatives. Most cannot afford to extend an 'open door' policy to students, i.e. they cannot be available to offer guidance and support as and when students require it. Instead, they must impose 'office hours' and set appointments for meeting with individual students. In this climate, there is a natural reduction in the one-to-one, face-to-face, individualised support that many students have found invaluable in the past and which many HE staff enjoy. In the 1990s, when student numbers in HE began to grow substantially and in many cases to double or more, strategies of working with larger numbers were devised (see the 'Teaching more students' series from Oxford Brookes University, reference in further reading below). One of the strategies of those of us who were involved in the development of work accompanying the books and the workshops attached to them (PCFC (Polytechnics and Colleges Funding Council) funded pre HEFCE (Higher Education Funding Council for England)) was to deal with large numbers imaginatively, and, when faced with an increase in numbers that seemed to jeopardise the particular

3

qualities of the teaching in that discipline, to identify those precious elements of the course delivery that must not be lost, retain them, then alter the rest, but always to ensure as good a quality of experience as possible and that students are encouraged to become autonomous, self-aware, reflective and creative learners. Some colleagues in Art and Design areas in particular retained the one-to-one relationship at all costs. Others insisted on developing structures that would funnel down so that large numbers could be taught for some relatively interactive information and argument sharing (lectures); smaller numbers could be taught and enabled in seminars or workshops to develop interaction, engagement and student support communities and, where necessary, some supportive one-to-one work would act as a surgery to those who needed further support or had problems in their learning. This is one model of retaining yet changing the nature of one-to-one, face-to-face tutoring. Another model is to ensure that there is at least one opportunity for this focused interaction, which is probably that of their first dissertation, project or thesis, where tutor and student can work together. In this book, we look at a range of such opportunities but are in no way trying to suggest that we can, if we wanted to, return to a master/pupil, utterly individual-focused relationship in learning in HE overall.

MEETING THE DEMANDS OF EMPLOYERS

One of the main aims of HE is to enable students to fulfil their learning potential, another is to match skilled workers to the developing and changing economy. Like others, the UK economy relies on a suitably skilled and qualified workforce for its success. Business and industry need 'employable' graduates to fill a wide range of professional roles, including leadership positions. Employers are increasingly vocal about what they see as a 'skills crisis' among university graduates. Poor literacy skills are a major component of this 'crisis' (Davies et al., 2006). However, a deficit in practical skills is also highlighted. As such, employers are calling for HE institutions to 'rethink traditional education models' in order to help improve recruitment and retention of graduate employees (Studd, 2006). As well as redesigning courses, the HE sector has responded with numerous initiatives, such as PDP, to ensure students gain 'transferable skills' (e.g. communication, presentation, report writing) during their university studies. Many universities also emphasise entrepreneurship and offer extra-curricular programmes that encourage students to develop the mind-set and skills necessary to set up and run their own businesses.

Some of the one-to-one roles discussed here, such as coaching and mentoring, are often specifically designed with the development of work-related skills in mind. These and others aim to engage the student with all aspects of their learning and much of this can be captured in terms of reflection and some evidencing in their Progress Report or Professional Development Profile.

Historically, teaching was often an interaction between master and pupil or a small group of pupils. The 'Oxbridge' model of individual tutoring is still held up as offering what has, for most of us, now become a luxury or a near impossibility, given the growing numbers of students with whom we work, whether lecturing or running seminars, now that HE is more available to a greater proportion of those able to benefit from it. For many of us starting to teach, there are very few opportunities to work one-to-one with students, but this can actually be one of the most rewarding kinds of learning and teaching. One-to-one we can engage with and match our thinking processes with one individual and encourage, enable and empower him or her to move on in their learning.

Being a supervisor, tutor, coach or mentor provides such opportunities for one-to-one work with a student. Relatively under-theorised and under-resourced, these roles still offer student and tutor the chance to identify each other's learning and teaching styles, agree (within the university or college boundaries and rules) on learning outcomes and upon ways of working together, perhaps using a learning contract, agendas, and reflective logs to accompany this work. Traditionally, the supervision of a dissertation or project has provided such opportunities for one-to-one work. Actually, ironically perhaps, even as student numbers have grown, with the possibly problematic loss of individual relationships, many of the opportunities for one-to-one work have also grown as the concern for student autonomy, independent problem solving, workplace and work-based learning, reflective development and generic and subject-specific skills have become more popular in HE. When working with students on independent learning or workplace, work-based learning, or in the development of their progress files/portfolios/PDP, we can act as coach, mentor and supervisor. Some of this supervising, coaching and mentoring takes place face-to-face, and sometimes through the interface of the computer with online learning, where we need to employ e-pedagogy and e-mentoring or moderating skills. Some students are engaged in resource-based learning that uses both face-to-face and online support. And students can act as mentors to each other too. Some of the most supportive, empowering strategies, which involve student mentors, have developed with 'supplemental instruction' and with schemes to support the first year experience, or 'buddy' schemes to enable students, particularly those from international origins or those with disabilities, to settle in and gain support.

One-to-one support and development is not confined to under-graduates. One of the greatest growth areas is that of postgraduate student numbers, and here, especially with the Masters dissertation, and the Ph.D., Ed.D. or Pr.D., supervision of individual work is the main learning and teaching activity.

Most HE teachers will be expected to supervise, tutor, mentor or coach students one-to-one at some time in their careers. For some of us it becomes our main contact with students.

In this book we look at, clarify, explore and share the skills, tensions, demands and joys of this one-to-one work, whether coaching, mentoring, tutoring or supervising. Early chapters focus on the skills and techniques needed to work with an individual student, matching the student's learning needs and learning styles with your own. Initially, this involves identifying learning outcomes and the routes to their achievement. Next, we proceed to work together productively over time until finally the student has developed the skills needed, can go on and learn to develop his or her own projects, manage them, act autonomously and independently and write the project report or dissertation/thesis. There are examples, reports or explorations of practice in each chapter, and clear advice is given about the processes of working with students as supervisor, coach, tutor and mentor or a similar role. Activities to undertake with students are also suggested. Each chapter considers ways of handling and overcoming difficulties that might arise, and further reading takes you on to other more in-depth or broader examples. We look at the variety of instances when one-to-one work takes place, the skills necessary, other learning, teaching and assessing skills, and we also look carefully at the interpersonal skills involved in these roles.

We consider ways of successfully developing strategies to engage, deal with and fulfil the different demands on us as tutors/supervisors/coaches/mentors in these differing situations. The situations range very widely. In one instance, we might be working to encourage someone to overcome difficulties. Perhaps they might be a dyslexic student or one who lacks confidence, whose writing skills, for instance, need support to enable him or her to be successful in their learning and articulation, and presentation of that learning. Or we might be empowering a high flying Ph.D. student to achieve an original, creative, coherent, Ph.D. thesis that makes a significant contribution to knowledge. Or we might be working with a student who is linking theorised academic university work with work-based learning, putting the theories into practice. In addition to 'further reading', each chapter ends with a list of useful websites.

We are all going to be involved at some time in supervising, coaching or mentoring students. This book should appeal to anyone involved in teaching or facilitating learning 'one-to-one', including all lecturers and tutors, learning support staff, advisers, library staff and other colleagues.

FURTHER READING

Davies, S., Swinburne, D. and Williams, G. (2006). 'Writing matters: the Royal Literary Fund report on student writing in higher education'. London: The Royal Literary Fund.

DfES (2003a). *The Future of Higher Education*. London: DfES.

DfES (2003b). *Widening Participation*. London: DfES.

Studd, S. (2006). SkillsActive's Higher Education Conference report. Available from: www.skillsactive.com/promotionlist/healthpromotion. Accessed 3 April 2006.

'Teaching More Students' series, Oxford Brookes University, Oxford. Available from: www.brookes.ac.uk/services/ocsld/books/teaching_more_students/index.html. Accessed 2 November 2007.

Chapter 1

An introduction to the skills and the roles

Coaching, mentoring, supervising and personal tutoring

Coaching, mentoring, supervising and personal tutoring are the main one-to-one relationships that link a student with others, and work to support the all round student experience in terms of a mix of both educational and personal development, in an educational context. Each of these roles has the underlying intention of supporting, facilitating, enabling and empowering students to develop so that they can produce their own autonomous, owned work and can develop as learners and then as employees and fully rounded people. At any point in our work with students in universities or colleges we may be expected to carry out any one or more of these roles working one-to-one with students. Each role carries with it some similar behaviours, which need to be developed, learned and practised by the coach, mentor, supervisor or personal tutor, including:

- engagement one-to-one with the student's needs and development;
- being able to provide a range of responses;
- observation;
- active listening skills;
- empathy;
- non-judgemental behaviour;
- organisation and planning;
- an ability to keep a professional distance;
- ability to give feedback;
- exhibiting the caring qualities that support students.

Some of the roles above might have slightly different meanings in the HE context to other meanings in business or even with younger students, and you might well find yourself undertaking each of them at different times in your professional career and, even, with the same student at different times, so it is useful to consider the differences, skills and kind of relationship needed for each.

COACHING

Coaching as a practice is a well-used tool within the business and personal development sectors, but is relatively new to HE settings. It is also often used in the worlds of sport and music. In terms of sports or musical talent, coaching as a form of development is a focused application of developmental suggestions that help individuals develop their sports, musical or other skills to the best of their ability. Singers and actors, as well as those in sports, might well have a personal coach, and this practice is based on the individual coach focused on working with the individual coachee, identifying his or her skills, needs and aims, developing a coaching plan that he or she agrees to, owns and wants to action, then working with the coachee to help him or her achieve it. Coaching has a slightly different meaning and use in the business world, but it is still about matching developmental support to the individual's skills and needs.

Coaching differs from traditional learning and teaching methods in that it is non-directive, encouraging the coachee to take charge of his or her own development – to identify and meet goals, improve skills, and develop discipline and motivation. The coach guides the coachee in dealing with current situations and in planning for the future. Coaching is increasingly popular in professional and vocational areas, as it mainly focuses on immediate, practical problems and concerns. In being learner-focused, it takes note of the specific skills and needs of the individual learner and presents opportunities as well as guidance along the trajectory of the learner's development. It offers potential use across HE, in the context of professional and personal development planning, actioning, reflecting and evaluating skills and attitudes for success in the discipline area and in work behaviour.

Successful coaching largely relies on the relationship-building, listening and questioning skills of the coach. Questioning is the main defining skill of coaching: the coach asks open questions that prompt the coachee to identify his or her own goals and strategies. The coach might gently push the coachee to come up with suggestions for action, but will not direct the coachee to 'the right answer'.

9

Coaching fits easily with the current HE emphasis on students as 'active learners', and the redefinition of lecturers as 'facilitators' or 'enablers' of learning. Coaching is an active learning task, requiring the student/coachee to identify his or her own aims and devise their own action plans. The HE teacher can easily acquire basic coaching skills through reading and practice. Specialised training is available for those who would like to develop their knowledge and skills further.

When might you be a coach?

Within HE there are a number of opportunities for coaching. Coaching can usefully take place at points of transition (Whittaker and Cartwright, 1997b), for example, the start of a new academic year or semester, the beginning of a supervisory relationship, or the establishment of a personal tutoring relationship. It is well-suited to use within tutorial sessions, where students' practical problems are traditionally dealt with. Distance-learning courses also provide a chance for coaching as, first, self-directed learning is already a requirement and, second, coaching by telephone and internet is successfully used in the private sector, so could be transferred to learning. Whether on- or off-campus, coaching can be used both with individual students and with groups. Students can also be guided to coach their peers. Group and peer coaching may be an effective option for HE settings, given teachers' limited time and resources.

Differences between coaching and mentoring

The terms 'coaching' and 'mentoring' are often used interchangeably. While there are similarities between the two practices (both involve one-to-one relationships and a focus on learning and development), coaching is different from mentoring in several key ways. First, coaching is often concerned with a specific problem, which the coach helps the coachee to define and overcome, or a skills need that the coach helps define and attain, while mentoring is concerned with monitoring and assisting an individual's development on a defined path, over a period of time. Second, the role of coach can be fulfilled by anyone who has sufficient knowledge and experience of coaching methods. The role of mentor, however, is usually occupied by someone who is more professionally or socially experienced than the mentee, often a person from the same professional or social group who has already travelled the journey.

MENTORING

Mentoring is commonly agreed to be a contested term but broadly encompasses a more experienced, possibly older, peer mentoring someone less experienced, to empower and enable them to develop necessary skills so that he or she can be effective as a learner and employee, depending on the context, and to enhance his or her own personal coping strategies, sense of self-worth and success. Much of the literature on mentoring focuses on its development in the context of working with underachieving young people in a school, further education or youth-work context. Other mentoring literature looks at its effectiveness in professional contexts where a kind of master–apprentice model is the most common.

Mentoring in HE

Mentoring in some HE contexts involves:

- working with an individual who wishes to learn some of the strategies you use in your study or job role;
- working with students on work-based learning placements who are learning about a job role;
- more senior staff mentoring those who would benefit from observing the skills in action and discussing the choices and perspectives involved in decisions and implementation of decisions.

With your overall support, it involves other students in:

- support for new students and those with particular needs, such as international students, students with disabilities;
- supplemental instruction (SI);
- peer assisted learning (PAL);

all of which are about students supporting the learning of other students.

Mentoring is both supportive and enabling. It can seem to derive from a deficit model, i.e. working with individuals on correcting problems and shortcomings, but, in the spirit of educational development, seeing it as enhancement and improvement, refining skills and developing new ones, would be a more caring and positive way of approaching mentoring. Training people to 'fit in' is another perception of the role of mentoring but, again, there are debates about this, and it should, the broad range of literature suggests, be seen not as social engineering and a reward for conformity to a dominant system but, rather, as a mode of development that empowers and enables both the mentee and the mentor.

There are some excellent examples of individual mentoring and also of group and peer mentoring in the HE literature. In peer mentoring, students mentor other students using supplemental instruction, where students further on in their study work with those new to the study, course or module, and where some students work with students with particular needs and issues such as English as a second language (ESL), disabilities or other learning needs. Mentors in the HE context can help ease the learning development and the student experience elements of entering and succeeding as a student.

Mentors are usually characterised by their relative seniority, whether they are one year further on in their study than those they are mentoring or hierarchically more senior, although mentoring is also possible when someone wishes to develop the skills for a new job role or responsibility. Mentees need to be able to benefit from the mentoring, PAL, SI or related activity, and both need to recognise it as a human relationship, an interaction with a professional intention within the context of the organisation. Mentoring students or new staff causes the mentor also to reflect on his or her own values, decisions, behaviours and skills, so be prepared to learn from the experience as you enable a student or new staff member to engage with development in the role with your modelling, support and guidance.

PERSONAL TUTORING

With increased numbers of students it is sometimes difficult for all students to have a personal tutor, but the tutor is, in effect, the first point of contact between student and the HE system and its expectations.

Personal tutors play an important part in the support structure offered in HE courses. They are a key contact point between the institution and the student. They can offer support at a more individual level than is sometimes possible within a formal teaching context, especially on large modular courses.

In their *Handbook for Personal Tutors* (1993), Sue Wheeler and Jan Birtle outline the primary aims of the PT as:

- to facilitate personal development of tutees;
- to monitor progress of tutees;

- to provide a link between students and university authorities;
- to be a responsible adult within the organisation in whom the student can confide;
- to intervene with the university authorities on behalf of their tutees.

In effect, this means that the personal tutor is in a mixture of a pastoral and an academic role with the tutees. He or she has some knowledge of the tutees' background needs and situation, their progress and their achievements or further academic needs, and can temper guidance in relation to this knowledge – the student's context. The tutor can refer students on to counselling and other student services and provide them with information about the processes of the university, both in support and academic terms. It is important for students to get to know their personal tutors very early in their studies and to maintain contact, possibly with a regular slot in the timetable, but certainly at points in the terms such as the beginning, half way and prior to assessment, then after assessment to consider results. As someone with an overview of the student in the context of the system – courses, regulations, facilities – the personal tutor can intervene and explain ways forward should the student have difficulties over their course, direction, choices, marks or need to resit exams. While the personal tutor might well hear of a whole range of difficulties as first point of contact, and provide support and empathy, he or she can intervene mainly to refer onwards to the appropriate university services in the case of financial and personal issues, but are not expected to solve these, rather, to provide support and information.

Ground rules and boundaries

As it is an extended role, students will need their tutor to develop and agree ground rules and boundaries so that the student knows when and how to contact the tutor, but is not too intrusive. Tutors, like supervisors, coaches and mentors need to be able to develop empathy, listening skills, sound time management and a good list of contacts for referral.

SUPERVISING

Supervising in a job context is most often a first-line management role, but in HE it usually starts when the student has a project, work placement, dissertation or thesis to write, i.e. an individualised, longer-term task that

13

a one-to-one relationship can support. Supervising resembles coaching and mentoring insofar as it aims to enable and support students, or others with whom you work, to develop their skills and achieve tasks. But it also has a sense of watching over, of working alongside someone and with them, enabling them to develop the kinds of skills and processes and to take these processes through to completion in products, and in skills development, so that students can use them in the future. Supervision also implies negotiation and dialogue. So that the one who is supervised, in this case the student, can develop his or her own version of the skills and processes, quite possibly of research or good learning practice, it is important that the supervisor negotiates choices and activities with students so that they understand these choices and the ways to go about solving problems, rather than being given answers and fixed solutions.

Good practices: interactions, ground rules

Supervision is a form of dialogue with the student where together you come to a shared understanding of what is to be done and why, how it was done, how well it was done and how to improve and/or identify what was successful and why. The ultimate aim of supervision is both a completed project and autonomous students who are empowered to carry out tasks and processes themselves, aware of the developing skills that they have and are continuing to gain. It is important in supervising:

- To have a mixture of a well-structured, well-organised set of ground rules and practice so that both the supervisor and student are aware of expectations and agreed behaviours.
- To develop mutual respect and trust and to be aware of, and work with, your differing needs and practices, valuing different skills and ways of learning but also learning from each other.
- To recognise that supervision is a form of teaching, and research or similar work under supervision, a form of learning. The supervisor will guide, offer ideas and reading, make comments on work produced, make suggestions and offer models for development, and the student needs to relate to and work with (not always accept every element of) that supervision and guidance.
- To establish and maintain a dialogue about issues, behaviours, decision making, action, planning, reflection, evaluation and

all stages of the working practice together. Supervision is a learning conversation with a student in which you develop agreed ways of working.

■ To also recognise that supervision is an authority relationship. However friendly and supportive a supervisor might be, he or she is also in a role of authority, which implies guidance, decision making, and some judgement on the quality of work.

Supervision probably works best when it is well organised, based on negotiation and dialogue, and well matched both to the demands of the activity – research in a university in line with the university and sector's expectations and standards – and the needs and learning approaches of the individual being supervised.

SKILLS ASSOCIATED WITH MENTORING, COACHING, SUPERVISION AND PERSONAL TUTORING

There are several necessary skills common to all of these roles – skills that enable you to engage with your students, hear their needs and issues and then to encourage them to develop, take responsibility, find out, plan, decide and act. Whatever your role it is important to:

■ listen;
■ empathise;
■ guide (but not order);
■ refer;
■ support;
■ reward;
■ help the student to develop independence.

Generic listening and one-to-one relationship skills

We will use the overall term 'teacher' in this context, but it is meant to comprise all and any of the roles – personal tutor, supervisor, coach or mentor.

Active listening – The teacher has to be totally present with the student, hearing and absorbing what the student says. Active listening is not just a matter of hearing the words spoken by the student – the teacher must also attend to the underlying meanings of the student's words, which includes picking up on emotional undertones (attending to tone of voice, noting the student's emphasis on certain words, and hearing the things that remain unsaid). The teacher can demonstrate active listening by actively summarising and reflecting back what the student has said. Listening can also be demonstrated through affirming noises ('mmm', 'yes') and attentive body language (smiling, nodding, leaning forward, eye contact). Frequently interrupting the student when they are speaking, or having to repeat questions because of 'lazy listening' (Parsloe, 1995: 121) will damage the teacher–student relationship. Active listening, however, will encourage the student to speak openly and to engage fully in the relationship.

Observing – The teacher needs to be attentive to the student's non-verbal communication, including facial expressions, posture, eye contact and body movements. Non-verbal communication may inform you of the student's feelings about the teacher–student relationship and of the student's commitment to, and progress with, learning. For example, a student who is angry and resentful may be tense and constrained in their movements, have clenched fists and gritted teeth; a bored student may fidget and yawn and avoid eye contact; a happy and motivated student may smile, lean forward towards the teacher, and nod often. However, body language is culturally specific and observations should always be checked verbally with the student to avoid misunderstanding. Mirroring the student's body language, e.g. rubbing your nose when the student does, crossing your legs, or lifting a cup at the same time, can be used to create rapport.

Empathy – The teacher must be able to recognise and understand the student's feelings *as if they were standing in the student's own shoes.* Try to see the situation as the student sees it, rather than from your own 'outsider' point of view. The teacher can stimulate empathy through active listening (see above), putting aside their own feelings and experiences, and by making statements that demonstrate they understand what the student is feeling (e.g. You're very happy about that!; You feel as if there's no hope; You're very confused about what to do next). Teachers must cultivate the ability to *genuinely* empathise with students, as the student will quickly be able to identify a teacher who is simply 'going through the motions' and this will have implications for the level of trust the student has in the teacher, in the relationship and in the learning and teaching process.

Non-judgemental – The teacher must put aside their own thoughts and experiences as far as possible and concentrate on entering the student's world and seeing things from his or her or his point of view. The teacher should be aware of their own prejudices and fears in order to avoid projecting these onto the student. For example, if the teacher worries about time management and berates themselves for this, they are likely to judge the student's poor time management in a negative way. The teacher should not jump to conclusions about what the student means, and should check their interpretation with the student if there is any doubt. Summarising what the teacher feels they have heard, and asking 'Is that right?' is a good way of checking understanding.

Authenticity – Teachers must aim to 'be themselves' during the learning and teaching relationship. They should guard against presenting themselves as 'the expert', thus masking their own uncertainties and vulnerabilities. Learning and teaching is a partnership process that has mutual benefit for all participants – the teacher and student are both likely to gain increased self-awareness, confidence and competence, as well as practical learning. Thus, learning and teaching work best if each party is as open and honest as possible and guard against 'playing a role' during learning and teaching sessions.

Relationship-building – A successful learning and teaching relationship enables the student to feel safe to express intellectual ideas and personal information, and to take the often difficult journey towards their goal. The teacher must create a confidential and stable environment for the student, work on building rapport with the student, clearly outline roles and expectations, and negotiate ways of working with the student.

Practising the above skills should help create an effective learning and teaching relationship.

For all the roles, it is important to have information about the ways the university or college conducts itself in terms of dates, assessment rules, information about Student Services, counselling, careers study support, chaplaincy and the various face-to-face and online agencies and mechanisms that can help students settle in in their first year and support them through to the completion of the undergraduate or postgraduate courses. Boundaries and clarity are important if you are going to be helpful to your student. Each role can have a tendency to slip into friendship or a more personally oriented relationship and this is a danger. It is a close but professional relationship and too much friendly involvement can cloud judgement and lead to expectations beyond the capacity of the tutor,

17

supervisor, coach or mentor. It also leads to a dependency that prevents the student from developing as an autonomous learner, able to find things out independently, make decisions and own their own learning.

Key skills throughout all of these roles

These can be seen to be:

- organisation;
- being informed about rules, regulations and referrals strategies and contacts;
- developing and agreeing ground rules and boundaries;
- empathising;
- supporting students to make decisions and plan, act, reflect and evaluate;
- supporting the development of informed, reasoned, planned and managed independence and autonomy.

Being effective as supervisors, coaches, mentors and tutors will partly depend on being adaptable to the learning styles and approaches of our different students, as well as to their needs and their disciplines. In the literature on pedagogy and learning styles or approaches, there are many experience-based and research-informed versions of students' diverse styles and approaches. One of the best known and most popular of these is the difference between deep, surface and strategic learning, which provides a useful insight on students' learning to keep in mind (developed in Chapter 6).

LEARNING STYLES AND APPROACHES

As we begin to think more about all forms of teaching and, particularly, about the expectations and needs of individual students, we might find it useful to revisit some of the work on learning approaches and learning styles. One of the best known of these is the differentiation between deep and surface strategies of learning. In one-to-one, face-to-face teaching, encouraging students to be deep learners by engaging in meaningful discussions can underpin a necessary committing to memory, which itself can be used to scaffold deeper learning. Students who go no further than rote learning will find it difficult to engage in the discussion necessary in one-to-one interaction, which can provoke and lead their comments and explanations. One-to-one or face-to-face teaching, then, can enable students to move from surface learning, which is often unrelated to other learning and lacks engagement with experiences in the real world, into deeper learning, where the meaning, usefulness and engagement can help students engage with discussions and interactions and active work.

'Deep', 'surface' and 'strategic' learning

Research into student learning shows that students acquire, retain and assimilate information best when a 'deep', rather than 'surface', approach is encouraged. 'Surface' learning is the passive memorising and recalling of material to meet external requirements such as assessment criteria. 'Deep' learning occurs when students are able to relate material to their own experience, and to engage in critical dialogue with the material to create new knowledge.

According to Brown:

'Surface' learning is:

- reproducing the knowledge given;
- accepting knowledge passively;
- focusing only on what you need to know for assessment purposes;
- not thinking about the wider context.

'Deep' learning is:

- wanting to understand the knowledge given, not just for assessment;
- questioning and challenging knowledge;
- relating knowledge to your own experiences and to the wider context;
- deconstructing arguments and advancing your own argument.

(adapted from Brown, 2004: 32)

Latterly, after Brown, 'strategic' learning was added to these two:

'Strategic' learning is:

- focusing on the directives and outcomes of the learning;
- ensuring the tasks are completed, grades achieved;
- not very interested in deep reflection and making meaning, rather in getting through the course successfully.

19

Students are likely to use a combination of these styles and, on the whole, it is important to encourage their deep learning, for understanding, meaning and retention, while not losing the focus on getting through the course successfully (strategic learning) as well.

 FURTHER READING

Brown, G. (2004). *How Students Learn*. London: RoutledgeFalmer.

Gulam, W. A. and Zulfiqar, M. (1998). 'Mentoring: Dr. Plum's elixir and the alchemist's stone'. *Mentoring & Tutoring*, 5 (3): 39–45.

Hall, J. (2003). *Mentoring and Young People: A literature review*. SCRE Research Report 114. Available from www.scre.ac.uk/resreport/pdf/114.pdf. Accessed 25 September 2007.

Parsloe, E. (1995). *Coaching, Mentoring and Assessing: A practical guide to developing competence*. London: Kogan Page.

Wheeler, S. and Birtle, J. (1993). *Handbook for Personal Tutors*. Buckingham: Open University Press.

Chapter 2

Coaching skills and supporting learners

Generic skills for one-to-one work

WHAT IS COACHING?

Coaching is a structured one-to-one learning relationship between coach and coachee, aimed at developing competence and improving performance in the coachee. Coaching is a practical helping tool – a tool that encourages 'the learning and development of an individual, [and] a process that involves change' (Brockbank and McGill, 2006: 2).

This chapter introduces staff in HE to basic coaching tools, which they can begin to integrate into their existing professional practice. However, the information outlined here is just one take on coaching, among a plethora of definitions and approaches that exist. Understandings and methods of coaching vary according to context, purpose and people involved. HE professionals intending to add coaching to their professional toolkit, must have a clear understanding of the coaching approach they are adopting and the philosophies underpinning that approach, alongside practical coaching skills. Suggestions for further reading at the end of this chapter encourage the reader to research the topic further.

MAIN FOCUS: ENCOURAGEMENT NOT DIRECTION

Although dictionaries often define coaching as 'training' or 'teaching', current coaching practice is less directive than these terms imply. The coach does not tell or show the coachee what to do. Rather, the coach encourages the coachee to take charge of their own learning, to set and achieve goals, and to develop the resources to fulfil their own potential.

Coaching employs skills common to other 'helping' professions, e.g. listening, observing, empathising and relationship-building. However, the main defining skill of coaching is questioning. An effective coach does not direct the coachee to the 'right' answer. Rather, he or she asks questions that encourage the coachee to realise their own solutions to problems, to define their own aims and strategies, and which motivate the coachee into action.

Coaching most often takes place in a working or learning environment, and concentrates on the coachee's practical, immediate concerns. The coach guides the coachee in dealing with a current situation, developing a skill they want to learn, or a behaviour they want to change. The coach also helps the coachee to plan for the future. However, the focus is always on the present, on taking action *now* to achieve short- and longer-term change.

KEY CHARACTERISTICS OF COACHING

Coaching is:

- a holistic process, looking at all aspects of an individual's life;
- usually undertaken one-to-one, or in small groups;
- a way of helping an individual to set and attain their own goals;
- a means of guiding an individual to recognise blocks to success;
- a way of increasing self-awareness;
- an effective tool for education, workplace and personal development.

COACHING IN HIGHER EDUCATION

Informal coaching takes place in HE every day, as teachers help students to set and achieve learning targets, to develop understanding and skills, and to take responsibility for their own learning. The current regard for 'student-centred' learning, which positions the student as an 'active' rather than a 'passive' participant in the learning and teaching process, makes coaching a valuable tool in HE classrooms and a natural part of the HE teacher's role.

However, more formalised coaching relationships – and training for the task – are beginning to gain popularity in university settings. Teachers are drawing on coaching models from the business world, and from the personal development sector, where structured coaching has enjoyed much growth and success in the past decade.

Coaching could potentially be undertaken in any area of HE, to improve the skill, performance and confidence of students and, of course, staff. But coaching is initially taking hold in professional and vocational areas such as nurse and teacher education, where work-based learning makes traditional learning and teaching methods untenable and new ideas welcome.

Coaching may at first seem like an extra burden for an already time-poor HE teacher but, performed effectively, coaching can ultimately save time, as it enables students to solve their own problems rather than looking to teachers for answers. The HE teacher becomes a *facilitator* of learning rather than providing students with the required knowledge. Students may at first feel resentful that teachers are not providing the answers they seek, however, they will quickly learn that they are required to take responsibility for their own academic career and will hopefully gain satisfaction, pride and confidence from doing so.

APPROACHES TO COACHING

Brockbank and McGill (2006) outline several approaches to coaching. These are: the **Functionalist approach**, which aims at improving individual performance to ensure efficient functioning of the status quo in an organisation or society, e.g. coaching staff to achieve qualifications in order to improve the organisation's working relationships, status and economic success; the **Engagement approach**, which focuses on the development needs of the coachee as a way of engaging them in the culture of an organisation or society, in order to maintain the status quo, e.g. coaching socially excluded young people to become 'employable'; the **Revolutionary approach**, aiming to change society through coaching individuals to change their beliefs and behaviour, e.g. Marxist or feminist 'consciousness raising' initiatives; and the **Evolutionary approach**, which focuses on the coachee's subjective experience, encourages responsibility for one's own learning, and invites the coachee to challenge dominant norms and structures, e.g. private life-coaching arrangements.

Brockbank and McGill discuss how these approaches vary in their usefulness to the HE context. They argue that the Functionalist approach should not be used because it discourages critical thinking and emphasises conformity and hierarchical relationships; the Engagement approach may be useful for engaging learners but is undesirable in that it encourages conformity rather than questioning; the Revolutionary approach is potentially useful as it encourages critical thought, but it often demands conformity to a 'grand narrative' rather than developing subjective under-standing; while the Evolutionary approach offers many opportunities because it fosters 'active' learning and encourages questioning of discip-linary knowledge, HE processes and social structures. However, the Evolutionary approach may maintain traditional individualism of academia and neglect the value of collective activity.

The advice and examples in this chapter are largely based on the Evolutionary approach to coaching. However, the basic coaching skills described below are used by all models.

THE UNITED STATES CONTEXT

While coaching is a relatively new concept in UK HE, the United States has seen a proliferation of 'academic coaches' in recent years. Most of these coaches work independently, targeting their services at students prepar-ing for HE as well as those already at university. Academic coaches 'guide and encourage students to open the doors, both academic and personal, barring the way to a higher education and personal growth' (Quinn, 2004). They help students clarify educational and career goals, improve study skills, and increase confidence. US schools and universities are begin-ning to employ academic coaches to augment traditional learning and teaching methods. These coaches are located mainly in 'study support' centres. Coaching activity is seen as separate from the teacher role. Aca-demic coach Sandy Maynard outlines the following benefits to educational establishments of employing a coach:

- increased engagement and attainment;
- decreased absenteeism;
- improved relationships.

Maynard suggests that students can benefit from:

- better self-esteem;
- more effective study skills;
- improved social skills;
- higher motivation;
- more satisfaction from education;
- increased sense of personal responsibility.

(adapted from Maynard, 2006)

Academic coaches are also employed to work with teachers in HE, helping them work through specific projects or changes, to reinvigorate their practice, and to build stronger learning and teaching and peer relationships.

COACHING AND STUDENT LEARNING IN THE CURRENT UK CONTEXT

As discussed elsewhere in this book, recent changes in UK HE have led to increases in student numbers, less directive learning and teaching methods and less contact time between teaching and student. Coaching can help to maximise the benefits of limited teacher–student contact time. For example, 'tutorials' could take the form of a series of structured coaching sessions, where the student identifies difficulties and areas for improvement and devises, and works through, a strategy for accomplishing their goals. Students could also be encouraged to work with peers who face the same difficulties or who are working on the same assignments, coaching one another. For distance-learning students, coaching via telephone or email is viable. Internet and telephone coaching is a popular method in private 'life coaching' relationships.

MEETING THE DEMANDS OF EMPLOYERS

Coaching could help to meet the graduate skills deficit that is increasingly highlighted by employers and professional bodies (see earlier in this book). Existing initiatives within universities, such as extra-curricular entrepreneurship workshops, are ideal sites for incorporating a coaching approach. Coaching models commonly used in business settings may be best for this purpose, as they familiarise students with the language and culture of the workplace. Students who undertake work placements as part of their HE course might also benefit from an integrated coaching programme, addressing both academic and work-based concerns.

TOWARDS A MORE HOLISTIC VIEW OF THE LEARNER

Coaching, especially from an Evolutionary approach (see above), encourages a view of the student as a rounded individual rather than an 'empty vessel' into which knowledge is poured. Evolutionary coaching is 'humanistic': focusing on and respecting the subjective experiences of the coachee and seeing the coachee as a person capable of self-directed growth.

25

Obviously, coaching HE students is undertaken within a defined framework, where attaining an educational qualification is the ultimate aim. Students-as-coachees must primarily focus on their educational goals, rather than on their aims and ambitions for the rest of their lives (e.g. transforming romantic and family relationships; improving their physical health). However, students' wider lives inevitably impact on their university learning and will almost always enter the coaching arena. Within an HE coaching environment, students can be encouraged to look at their lives in holistic terms (e.g. how time for study can be negotiated within their home, or with an employer), but academic concerns must be their central focus. If a student's wider life is negatively impacting on their studies, or the student seems unable to manage competing pressures, the teacher should refer the student for specialist advice and guidance (e.g. to welfare or counselling services) rather than allowing these issues to dominate coaching sessions. However, the coachee is likely to experience wider personal development during coaching sessions. While identifying and working towards goals, the coachee will inevitably become more self-aware and gain increased clarity about their situation and life.

'Holism' often implies a focus on emotional and spiritual life and relationships. Coaching can certainly help students in HE to develop connections with other people, including peers, tutors and employers. Coaching works through relationships, either one-to-one or in a small group. Effective coaching depends on an effective relationship between coach and coachee. As such, the relationship itself, and the coachee's wider relationships, deserve attention within the coaching programme. Coaching provides a concentrated opportunity for the student to develop rapport and trust with another individual. This relationship-building may be as valuable to the coachee as the process of goal setting and attainment. Of course, within this relationship, the coach must act with the utmost ethical propriety, and must not abuse the coachee's trust. The coaching relationship must be an equal one, providing the opportunity for mutual respect and growth. Through coaching, the HE teacher may learn as much about relationship-building as the student.

Moving to a holistic model may be difficult for some HE teachers, given that academia is traditionally based on *fragmentation* of the self, and a focus on *intellectual* life, to the large neglect of other aspects of an individual's experience. However, coaching does fit in with current academic shifts to more personal forms of knowledge-making – a recognition of the 'knowing self' as socially located, and as a simultaneously intellectual, emotional, physical and spiritual being.

'DEEP' AND 'SURFACE' LEARNING

Tasks that require active student participation are likely to lead to deep learning. Examples of active learning methods include group discussion, problem solving and designing and conducting research.

Coaching is an active learning task, as it requires the student to construct their own questions, supply their own answers and solve their own problems, rather than relying on material they are given by a teacher or have read in a book.

Kolb's learning cycle is often quoted in coaching texts to illustrate the need for, and benefits of, coaching. Kolb's model suggests that learning primarily occurs through experience. However, several stages must be gone through if learning is to take place: *having an experience* leads to *thinking / reflecting* on the experience, *then drawing conclusions* from the experience, and *planning the next step* – the next step is a new experience and so the cycle continues. Atherton (1999) provides a good account of the process as it relates to coaching. Coaching leads the coachee through all stages of the cycle. Atherton states that perhaps the greatest benefit of coaching, in terms of Kolb's learning cycle, is that it encourages the coachee to *reflect* on their experiences, to identify what works and what doesn't work for them. In HE, coaching can lead students to, among other things, identify their personal learning style, assess their performance with essays and exams, and examine their study strategy to see what can be improved.

OPPORTUNITIES FOR COACHING

The teacher–student relationship in HE provides a number of opportunities for coaching. Whittaker and Cartwright (1997b) suggest that points of change and transition may provide the best times to initiate coaching. For teachers and students these times include:

- start of a new course or module;
- start of a new academic year or semester;
- beginning of a supervisory relationship, e.g. for a dissertation or thesis;
- establishing a personal tutoring relationship;
- after a specific event, e.g. the student has failed an exam.

However, an experienced coach is able to spot other coaching opportunities during their daily work. In HE, for example, a teacher might encounter a student having difficulty with time management; another student might be worried about slipping grades; or a group of students might seek the lecturer's guidance on how to work together on a joint project. As already suggested, coaching can take place in 'tutorial' sessions, where many of these problems would traditionally be handled.

As also mentioned above, distance-learning courses provide a valuable opportunity for coaching, as online courses require the teacher to shift to a less directive, and more facilitative, role. Coaching allows the teacher, among other things, to encourage self-directed learning, to check that the 'virtual' students are feeling comfortable and confident with the course and to identify any problems, and to structure online student discussions (Murphy *et al.*, 2005).

DIFFERENCES BETWEEN COACHING AND MENTORING

The words 'coaching' and 'mentoring' are often used interchangeably. This blurring is understandable given that there *are* similarities between the two practices: both involve one-to-one relationships, are common in education and the workplace, and are concerned with helping an individual to learn and develop. Adding to the confusion is the fact that, in many organisational settings, mentors often undertake coaching and vice versa (Cox, 2003).

However, coaching is different from mentoring in several key ways: traditionally, mentoring is concerned with mapping an individual's development over a period of time, and examining stages and turning points in that journey (Brockbank and McGill, 2006). The mentor role is commonly undertaken by someone who is perceived to have more 'experience' than the mentee, either in professional or social terms. The mentor often occupies the same professional or social group as the mentee, but is someone who has already travelled the journey that the mentee is about to embark upon.

By contrast, coaching is concerned with a problem, which the coach helps the coachee to define and overcome. The role of coach can be undertaken by anyone, given adequate knowledge of coaching methods. The coach does not have to be 'senior' to the coachee, or have more experience or expertise. Coaching is not about guiding the coachee on a particular, already defined, journey, but is about enabling the coachee to identify and undertake their own journey by first defining the desired goal or destination.

DIFFERENCES BETWEEN COACHING AND COUNSELLING

Although coaching can be enhanced by drawing on counselling skills and techniques (see below), coaching and counselling are entirely separate fields of practice. The aim of counselling is to help clients deal with *emotional* issues that are affecting their lives and to undertake emotional growth. Counsellors are trained to manage clients' emotional distress and are, therefore, equipped to guide clients in exploring deep-seated personal issues. Counsellors have recognised counselling and therapy qualifications, are usually members of a professional counselling body, and work within strict professional frameworks.

Coaches might help coachees deal with personal issues, as well as learning and work-related goals, and might facilitate the coachee's personal growth. However, coaching focuses on *practical* rather than emotional changes that can be made in order for the coachee to lead a more effective life. Unless they are also qualified counsellors, coaches should not lead coachees into discussion of emotional concerns or respond to a coachee's need to talk at emotional depth. A coachee's practical problems will inevitably have emotional aspects but exploring these is not the coach's responsibility. The coach can acknowledge the emotional situation of the coachee in general terms (e.g. 'You sound angry about that'; 'I can see that causes you frustration') in order to demonstrate good listening. However, the focus should quickly return to practical matters. If the coach feels a coachee requires counselling instead of, or in addition to, coaching, the coach can refer the coachee on to a specialised service.

COACHING SKILLS AND TECHNIQUES

The coaching relationship

Coaching, like other one-to-one work, involves building and maintaining effective relationships. The coaching relationship is based on principles of partnership and equality, where coach and coachee are co-participants. Thus, the coaching relationship destabilises the traditional teacher–student hierarchy. In HE, the coaching relationship can be seen as analogous to the current approach to academic research, where research 'subjects' are viewed as 'companions', and the researcher is 'co-learner' rather than 'expert' (Coe, 2004). The coach can build a strong coaching relationship through establishing ground rules and procedures (e.g. via a coaching contract), working to establish rapport with the coachee, and displaying good listening skills (see below for discussion).

Coaching contracts

Brockbank and McGill advise that 'no coaching should begin without an agreed contract' (2006: 174). The coaching contract sets out the ground rules of the coaching relationship in order to ensure each party is clear about their roles and responsibilities. The contract outlines the coach's

---

COACHING CONTRACT

We are about to begin a coaching process.

We will meet weekly for ___ weeks and then review the process. The first session will be on _____ and will last ___ minutes.

OUR AGREEMENT

Client

I, [name]_____ , agree to:

1   Be on time for each coaching session.

2   Prepare for each session by completing any worksheets or exercises the coach gives to me and by carrying out my agreed actions from the previous session.

3   Give at least 24 hours' notice if I need to reschedule a coaching session.

4   Accept that I am absolutely responsible for my own actions, and that I initiate this coaching relationship on that basis.

5   Agree that I'll raise with my coach, without delay, anything that I'm unhappy about in our coaching relationship.

6   Remember that every coaching session is totally confidential and that it is in my best interests to be honest and open with my coach.

7   I agree that I want to move forward in my life and learning and I will give the coaching process my absolute commitment.

Signed   _____

Date   _____

---

usual practices and procedures but allows room for the coachee to negotiate their own terms. The contract should reflect the egalitarian nature of the coaching relationship and so should not be imposed on a coachee; the contract must be preceded by discussion and must reflect mutual agreement.

An example of a coaching contract (based on the contract used by Maria Antoniou in her private coaching practice) is shown on these two pages.

Within HE settings other things might have to be added to the contract, e.g. details of the course or project the coaching relates to, and any

---

Coach

I, [name]_____, will demonstrate my commitment to you and our coaching relationship by:

1 Being on time for each coaching session and fully prepared.

2 Giving you at least 24 hours' notice if, for any reason, I have to cancel a coaching session.

3 Maintaining 100 per cent confidentiality with you unless required by law to disclose anything you tell me.

4 Being totally focused on your needs and committed to supporting and encouraging you to take the steps you have identified to meet your ambitions and goals.

5 If at any time we mutually agree that life coaching is not the most appropriate way forward for you at this time in your life, we will work together to determine the termination of sessions and/or referral to another source of support.

6 If at any time I identify that you are not fully committed to your goals and agreed actions, I will raise this with you so that we can determine the most appropriate course of action.

7 I agree to coach you to the best of my ability, with 100 per cent of my energy and commitment.

Signed _____

Date _____

This is a professional agreement between two people and is not a legally binding document.

particular issues regarding disclosure of information and confidentiality. A Head of Department, Course Leader or other academic colleague may have to countersign the contract, depending on the needs of particular settings and the agreements reached.

Models of coaching

As already outlined, coaching is essentially based on (1) defining goals, and (2) moving towards achieving them. Several models have evolved for undertaking this process. The GROW model – developed by John Whitmore (1996) – is one of the most frequently used approaches in current coaching practice. GROW is a performance-oriented model, aimed at maximising an individual's potential. GROW is an acronym:

G – establish the goal;
R – examine the reality of the situation;
O – consider the options available;
W – confirm will to act; decide what will happen.

Setting goals

Goal-setting often employs another acronym: goals must be SMART. SMART goals are:

S – specific; involving tangible outcomes, methods and dates;
M – measurable; easy to tell when goal has been achieved;
A – achievable; possible within given timeframe and conditions;
R – realistic; possible within personal capabilities and limitations;
T – time-specific: must have a target date for achievement.

Other helpful goal-setting acronyms include: MMM – *measurable, manageable, motivational* – and RAW – *realistic, attainable, worthwhile* (Brockbank and McGill, 2006).

The GROW model in practice: an example coaching session

The GROW model provides a structure for the coaching session. This structure can be repeated at every session, with the coach asking similar questions and the coachee providing different answers as he or she progresses with their learning and development.

Goal-setting – The coachee may come to coaching with a definite sense of what they want to achieve, they may have a vague feeling that 'things aren't right and need to change', or be somewhere in between. The coach's first task is to help the coachee clarify their goals. Following the 'SMART' model above, goals must have a timeframe and measurable outcomes attached. The coach asks questions such as:

- What do you want to achieve?
- Is this a long- or short-term goal?
- By which date do you want to have achieved this goal?
- How will you know when you've achieved it?
- What resources do you have that will help you achieve your goal?

In an example session, a second-year undergraduate student has come to the coach for help with her study skills and time management, and the ultimate dream of achieving a first class degree. Her long-term goal (achieving a first) is clearly time-bounded and measurable. However, her more immediate goals regarding study practices are less easy to define. The coach will first listen to the student's initial account of her situation. He or she will then guide the student to set specific goals and to prioritise them. Between them, coach and coachee will agree which goal or goals to concentrate on during their subsequent sessions.

Examining reality – Once the goal is established, the coach needs to obtain a fuller picture of the coachee's present situation. The coach will ask questions that draw out the details of the current context. During this stage, the coach will also be looking to assess whether the coachee's goal is realistic, given their wider circumstances and resources. The coach may use the following phrases and questions:

- Tell me more about . . .
- I'm not quite clear about . . .
- So, at the moment you're . . .
- Are there any other circumstances affecting your present situation?

33

Pursuing the above example, the coach will encourage the student to talk about barriers to more effective study skills and time management, including the effects of her part-time job, an active social life with too many late nights, her dyslexia, and her lingering doubt that she is on the wrong degree programme. Unless a goal seems wholly unrealistic (e.g. the coachee is planning to write two 3,000-word essays in 24 hours, having done no research) the coach will not make a value judgement about the coachee's ability to achieve her goals, but will voice the potential barriers, as the coachee has expressed them, and assert the need to devise strategies for overcoming these barriers.

Considering options – At this stage, the coach will encourage the coachee to examine how she will achieve her goals. They will push the coachee to suggest numerous possibilities for action. During the options stage, the coach must be tough, motivating the coachee to identify more and more possibilities. The coach will keep pushing the coachee for options even when the coachee feels she has exhausted all avenues. The coach will not suggest options but will encourage the coachee to devise her own. The coach will ask questions such as:

- How will you achieve this goal?
- What else can you do to achieve your goal?
- What are three more options available to you?
- If you were advising a friend in this situation, what would you suggest they do?

The example second year student above may consider, among other things, finding a part-time job that better fits in with her university time-table; restricting her nights out to weekends only; officially notifying the institution of her dyslexia and achieving the necessary adjustments and support; and speaking to a careers counsellor about her feelings of being on the wrong course. The coach will then help the coachee work through one identified option at a time, or more than one depending on realistic manageability.

Confirm will to act; devise action plan – In the final section of the coaching session, the coach will make sure the coachee is committed to taking action and will guide the coachee to come up with a strategy for achieving her goal. The coach must again be tough with the coachee in order to ensure the coachee knows she is required to take control of her own development rather than being a passive recipient of coaching. The coach will ask:

- How much do you want to achieve this goal on a scale of one to ten?
- What would it take to make your motivation ten out of ten?
- What's the first step you will take? How will you do this?
- What will you do next?
- After you've done that, what else will you do?
- When will you know you've reached your goal?

In the example session, the coach will ask the student what she can realistically do during the next week. The student may suggest: informing her friends she is only socialising at the weekends and turning down any invitations she receives; searching for a new job in the local paper and asking friends if they know of any vacancies; finding out who to contact in order to notify the institution of her dyslexia, contacting them and making an appointment; making an appointment to see a careers counsellor; setting aside two hours each evening to review lecture notes and to begin work on her assignments.

Ending the coaching session

The coach will write down the action plan as the coachee devises it and will then read the action plan back to the coachee and seek confirmation that the coachee will enact the plan within a specified time frame. The coach and coachee will agree on what the coachee will have achieved by the next session. The coach will give the coachee positive feedback for their learning and development during the session.

The coaching environment

Coaching ideally takes place in a space where both coach and coachee feel at ease. Interruptions from outside will be minimised: the door will be shut, telephones will be switched off or diverted, answer machine volume will be turned down, a do-not-disturb sign will be placed on the door. This will signal to the coachee that their learning and development is a serious matter, deserving focused time and attention. Even if coaching takes place on the telephone or by email, effort should be made by both parties to prevent interruptions.

Where the coach and coachee are meeting in person, the seating should ideally be arranged so that the two parties are facing one another without a barrier, such as a desk, between them. The aim is to create an atmosphere that is relaxed but business-like and in which both parties feel comfortable.

Individual and group coaching

While this chapter mainly sets out procedures for one-to-one coaching, the structures and skills described here can also be used with groups. The benefits of group coaching are that more coachees can enjoy the benefits of coaching, and that coachees can support one another's development and potentially develop coaching skills themselves. The disadvantages of group coaching are that each coachee will have less individual attention and that the coach must work harder to establish ground rules and a sense of safety for the group and to monitor the relationships between various group members as well as between themselves and each coachee.

Group coaching may be an effective option for HE settings, however, given teachers' limited time and resources. As suggested above, running tutorials as peer coaching sessions would help students to be more self-directed in their learning and to develop their relationships with peers. If students are required to undertake peer coaching, at least one training session on coaching skills is required, including ample time for practice. All participants in peer coaching relationships must work by mutually agreed ground rules and must take responsibility for monitoring their own learning as both coaches and coachees. The teacher-coach will still need to monitor progress of student-coachees, e.g. by gathering copies of action plans at the end of each session, and undertaking regular reviews with either the whole group or with individuals.

Skills required for coaching

> There is an old saying that God gave us two eyes, two ears but only one mouth so that we could look and listen four times as much as we speak.
>
> (Parsloe, 1995: 121)

The core skills required for coaching are similar to those required in other 'helping' professions. Core skills include:

- active listening;
- observing;

- empathy;
- non-judgement;
- authenticity;
- relationship-building.

These skills are discussed in an earlier chapter. However, the main defining skill of coaching is questioning.

Questioning

Parsloe states that the use of questioning within education originated in Ancient Greece where Socrates found it an effective method for facilitating student learning: 'Questioning, Socrates advocated, was the appropriate technique to help the student discover for themselves what they needed to know' (Parsloe, 1995: 55). An effective coach asks questions that motivate the coachee into action. Questions are open (asking 'what?', 'why?', 'how?') rather than closed (requiring a 'yes' or 'no' answer); they are also short and focused, rather than long and multi-faceted. Effective coaching questions encourage the coachee to clearly visualise their goals and the path towards achieving them (What do you want to achieve? How will you know when you've achieved it? How will you get there? What's stopping you from reaching your goal?). A good coach asks questions that keep the coachee on track to their goals and avoid diversions. Also, a good coach does not ask leading questions that try to push the coachee into specific goals and actions. Questions must be delivered in a firm but encouraging manner; the coach must never be aggressive or patronising. The coachee's answers must be respected as the 'right' ones. However, the coach can gently 'push' with more challenging questions if the coachee seems low on ideas or motivation (Why do you want to achieve this goal? On a scale of one to ten how motivated are you to achieve this goal? Why isn't it ten? What other ideas do you have for achieving this goal?). However, remaining silent when the coachee is struggling, rather than asking another question, will often encourage further expression of thoughts and feelings.

Alongside the above skills, an effective coach will also be able to recognise and respond to different learning styles; acknowledge and reward achievement and success; and gain the coachee's respect and commitment. The coach must be able to give effective feedback, to build the coachee's confidence and to motivate the coachee to become self-directed in their learning.

Tackling resistant coachees

An effective coaching relationship depends on full commitment and participation from the coachee. The coachee cannot passively receive coaching,
but must be an equal participant in the relationship. The coachee must be
willing to learn and to take responsibility for their learning, they must
be willing to change existing ways of thinking and behaving, willing to
assess their abilities and performance honestly, able to listen to feedback,
and able to face their own weaknesses openly (Whittaker and Cartwright,
1997b: 57).

Coachees may display their resistance through body language (arms
folded, frowning, refusal to make eye contact), verbal signals (sighing,
tutting, challenging the coach at every opportunity), or withdrawal
from activity (not completing agreed actions, failing to attend sessions).
Faced with a resistant coachee, the coach can suggest a review of the
coaching relationship. The review session will give the coachee a chance
to voice their feelings about coaching. Resistance may be born from
vulnerabilities, including fear of change, fear of failure and fear of success. Therefore, the coach needs to approach the review positively and
supportively, ensuring the coachee feels they are an equal participant
in the session and not as if the coachee is being 'told off' for their
resistance.

During the review, the coach might ask questions such as 'What do
you think is working well in this relationship?', 'What is working less
well'?, 'How can we improve things?'. Although the coach might have
their own answers to these questions, the coachee's answers must take
priority and provide the basis for subsequent action. For example, if after
lengthy discussion, the coachee is insistent they do not want to continue
with coaching, the final decision must be theirs. Making coaching compulsory within HE is therefore undesirable. However, where compulsory
coaching is delivered, the coach should ensure the process is as coachee-
led as possible.

If, during the review, the coachee provides the coach with negative
feedback, and blames the coach's attitude or behaviour for their own feelings of resistance, the coach must aim to listen openly and objectively and
carefully consider the coachee's accusations. The coach might then reflect
on the information themselves, or discuss the situation confidentially with
a coach trainer, a colleague or their manager.

IDEAS FOR COACHING ACTIVITIES

The Wheel of Life

The Wheel of Life is a popular coaching tool which the coach can use with the coachee at the 'Reality' stage of the coaching session (see above). The Wheel of Life helps the coachee gain perspective on all their activities and to gain an accurate sense of which areas of their life they give most time and energy to and which areas receive least attention. In HE, the Wheel of Life may help students to examine the amount of time they allocate to studying and to assess whether they give too much or too little to this area of life in relation to their wider goals and to other life demands. An important aspect of the Wheel of Life is that it reminds the coachee to allocate time to relaxation and leisure, areas of life that can often become neglected when an individual is faced with a large workload and is experiencing stress.

The coach can either use an existing Wheel of Life template (Figure 2.1, or see Mind Tools, 2006) or can guide the coachee to draw their own on a blank sheet of paper. In drawing a Wheel of Life the coachee begins with a circle, divided up by straight, bisecting lines into at least eight segments, so that it looks like a wheel. The segments are then labelled with areas of the coachee's life, e.g. university, job, partner, family, social life, leisure, health and fitness. The coachee then marks a dot in each section to indicate the amount of time and energy they give to that section of their life. A dot near the centre of the circle indicates little or no time

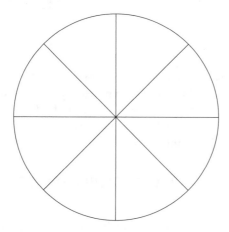

■ FIGURE 2.1   Wheel of Life template

is given to that area, a dot on the outer edge of the circle shows that that area of life occupies most or all of the coachee's time. The coachee can then connect the dots in each section of the circle. If the connected dots make a perfect circle, the coachee's life is perfectly balanced. If the circle is more wobbly, the coachee can see which areas of life are receiving most and least attention.

List making

List making can be used in group coaching, in internet coaching or in one-to-one coaching when the coachee feels they have run out of things to say and/or finds it easier to articulate their thoughts through writing instead of speaking. List making can be used at any stage of the coaching process but is most useful when considering 'Options'. Making a list also helps the coachee to focus on the reasons why they want to achieve certain goals and thus can motivate them to make changes.

The coach simply asks the coachee to write the numbers one to ten in the margin of a blank piece of paper, and then to list, as quickly as possible, whatever comes to mind in answer to a certain question or topic. The aim of list making is to bypass the coachee's inner critical voice, which may otherwise censor their responses, and to help the coachee recognise what they truly think and feel. Possible headings for lists are: Ten ways I could improve my time management; Ten reasons I want to gain a first class degree; Ten things I could do this week to help me find a new job; Ten ways I could say 'no' when friends ask me to engage in social activities on a weeknight.

Other activities

Coaches can also use tools and activities drawn from non-coaching sources to augment their coaching. For example, many of the activities provided in learning and teaching guides (e.g. the '53 ways' book series published by Technical & Educational Services Ltd – see reference list for information) are potentially useful.

EVIDENCE FOR THE EFFECTIVENESS OF COACHING

Coaching organisations and academic researchers – especially academics from psychology and business disciplines – have, in recent years, embarked on numerous projects aimed at studying the effectiveness of coaching on coachees' learning and development, on organisations, and on wider society. There is now a growing body of evidence on which to base coaching practice, and which can be used to validate new and existing coaching programmes.

The *International Journal of Evidence Based Coaching and Mentoring* is at the forefront of the turn towards evidence-based practice. The journal is an ideal resource for HE practitioners and students as it is edited from within a UK university (Oxford Brookes) and contains research articles written and reviewed to rigorous academic standards. The journal is free-access and available online (see references section for details).

TRAINING FOR COACHES

In early 2006, the UK government commissioned ENTO (a UK standards setting body) to undertake a consultation towards the development of national training standards and qualifications for coaching and mentoring. But, as yet, there is no central regulatory body for coaching in the UK, no nationally recognised occupational standards for coaches, nor any uniform system of accreditation.

Training and development for coaches can, at present, be undertaken via a variety of routes. There are numerous independent organisations offering training in coaching skills, some of which have courses accredited by UK universities or learning bodies such as the Open College Network (OCN). In the UK, such courses include those available from *The Coaching Academy*, *Achievement Specialists*, and the *Oxford School of Coaching and Mentoring* (see resources section). However, training with independent organisations can be expensive and courses are targeted primarily at the business sector. Several educational institutions also offer coaching courses at various levels, including Certificate, Diploma and Masters, for example, Newcastle College and Oxford Brookes University. Coach training can also be undertaken via the Chartered Institute of Personnel and Development (CIPD).

Although understanding of basic coaching skills can be acquired from a book or website, some formal training or development is advisable for those who use coaching on a regular basis, or work with 'vulnerable' people: 'There is a potential for damage to vulnerable clients from either coaches who "tell" or coaches who "pathologize"' (Brockbank and McGill, 2006: 238). In the absence of inexpensive, locally based coaching training, a short introductory counselling skills course, offered by most FE colleges and some universities, can provide the opportunity to acquire understanding of theoretical models that underpin much coaching practice (e.g. humanistic psychology) and to practise key skills necessary for coaching (e.g. active listening). Another option is to form a peer learning group with colleagues, practising coaching skills on one another, discussing coaching work with students, and reflecting on your own learning.

CONCLUSION

This chapter has provided a general introduction to coaching approaches and skills, and suggested ways that coaching might be used in HE. Coaching potentially offers an alternative to traditional learning and teaching methods – one that encourages self-directed learning and the forging of more effective studying and working practice. As coaching enables individuals to identify and meet their goals, build better relationships, and develop discipline and motivation, the value of coaching to students, teachers, HE institutions and society is potentially great.

 FURTHER READING

Atherton, T. (1999). *How to be Better at Delegation and Coaching*. London: Kogan Page.

Brockbank, A. and McGill, I. (2006). *Facilitating Reflective Learning Through Mentoring & Coaching*. London: Kogan Page.

Brown, G. (2004). *How Students Learn*. London: RoutledgeFalmer.

Coe, S. (2004). 'Exploring a personal experience of coaching'. Available from: www.business.heacademy.ac.uk/resources/reflect/conf/2004/coe/index. html. Accessed 3 April 2006.

Cox, E. (2003). 'The contextual imperative: implications for coaching and mentoring'. *International Journal of Evidence Based Coaching and Mentoring*, 1 (1): 9–22.

Davies, S., Swinburne, D. and Williams, G. (2006). *Writing Matters: The Royal Literary Fund report on student writing in higher education*. London: The Royal Literary Fund.

DfES (2003a). *The Future of Higher Education*. London: DfES.

——— (2003b). *Widening Participation*. London: DfES.

Maynard, S. (2006). 'Academic coaching'. Available from: www.sandymaynard. com/academic.html. Accessed 3 April 2006.

Mind Tools (2006). 'Mind tools'. Available from: www.mindtools.com. Accessed 17 July 2006.

Murphy, K. L., Mahoney, S. E., Chen, C., Mendoza-Diaz, N. V. and Yang, X. (2005). 'A constructivist model of mentoring, coaching and facilitating online discussions'. *Distance Education*, 26 (3): 341–66.

Parsloe, E. (1995). *Coaching, Mentoring and Assessing: A practical guide for developing competence*. London: Kogan Page.

Quinn, E. (2004). Academic coach's website. Available from: http://erika quinn.com. Accessed 3 April 2006, no longer available.

Studd, S. (2006). SkillsActive's Higher Education Conference report. Available from: www.skillsactive.com/promotionlist/healthpromotion. Accessed 3 April 2006.

Technical & Educational Services Ltd (no date). 'Technical & Educational Services Ltd'. Available from: www.53books.co.uk/index.html. Accessed 17 July 2006.

Whitmore, J. (1996). *Coaching for Performance*. London: Nicholas Brearly.

Whittaker, M. and Cartwright, A. (1997b). *32 Activities on Coaching and Mentoring*. Aldershot: Gower.

Useful journals

International Journal of Evidence Based Coaching and Mentoring: www.brookes.ac.uk/ schools/education/ijebcm/home.html.

International Journal of Mentoring and Coaching: www.emccouncil.org/frames/ journalframe.htm.

Organisations offering coaching courses and qualifications

Please note: neither the author of this chapter, nor the editors or publishers of this book endorse any organisations or courses mentioned here. Addresses are given for information only.

Achievement Specialists: www.achievementspecialists.co.uk/.

Chartered Institute of Personnel and Development: www.cipd.co.uk.

Newcastle College: www.ncl-coll.ac.uk/.

Oxford Brookes University, Westminster Institute of Education: www.brookes. ac.uk/schools/education/.

Oxford School of Coaching and Mentoring: www.oscm.co.uk.

The Coaching Academy: www.the-coaching-academy.com/.

Chapter 3

Personal tutoring

The role of a personal tutor is a vital one, but new academic staff can sometimes take it on without being entirely sure what is expected of them. This chapter is intended to help you to:

- clarify your own views on the role, and consider how these may fit with student expectations as well as institutional policies and processes;
- develop your confidence in the role of personal tutor and your ability to support your students effectively;
- explore some common issues that can arise in tutorials and consider ways of dealing with them;
- understand the range of specialist support services that are likely to be available, and know when and how to refer students to such support.

WHAT DO PERSONAL TUTORS DO?

Personal tutors play an important part in the support structure offered on all HE courses, representing a key contact point between the institution and the student. They can offer support at a more individual level than is sometimes possible within a formal teaching context, especially on large modular courses.

In their *Handbook for Personal Tutors* (1993), Sue Wheeler and Jan Birtle outline the primary aims of the PT as:

- to facilitate personal development of tutees;
- to monitor progress of tutees;

- to provide a link between students and university authorities;
- to be a responsible adult within the organisation in whom the student can confide;
- to intervene with the university authorities on behalf of their tutees.

Since then, some expectations might have changed and others have received more attention and there has been a renewed understanding of the value of a stable point of contact with an individual tutor.

Students arrive at university with diverse attitudes and expectations. They might have succeeded easily at school and then find it hard to adapt to the more independent atmosphere of university. Alternatively, they

---

 **ACTIVITY**

Expectations

The term 'personal tutoring' is interpreted in widely disparate ways, and this can lead to problems if staff and students bring different expectations to the relationship. It is helpful to be aware of your own assumptions and whether they are appropriate to current circumstances and constraints.

a Think about your own experience as a student of receiving personal tutoring (or similar academic/pastoral support):

- What was the most positive aspect?
- What could have been improved?
- What qualities did your tutor(s) bring to the role?

b How would you like your students to perceive you as a personal tutor? (E.g. friend, mentor, parent, supervisor, counsellor . . .)

- Is this achievable?
- What are the obstacles?
- What problems might be associated with students perceiving you in this way?

There are no right answers here. The important thing is to be aware of your own preferred tutoring style, and where this might conflict with other expectations or the demands of a particular situation. Advice on boundaries between professional roles is included later in this guide.

might have experienced academic failures in the past and struggle with low self-confidence. A surprising number, especially in the early months, will assume that everyone else is coping well and that any difficulties they experience must mean they are on the wrong course or even unsuited to HE as a whole.

As a personal tutor, you have the opportunity to put these anxieties into perspective and guide the student through any initial difficulties. You can help to establish realistic expectations, encourage effective study patterns, and generally contribute to a more fulfilled student experience, by offering continuity throughout their degree. In some institutions, this support may continue beyond the programme, with tutors writing references or offering informal advice long after graduation.

Whatever the variations in individual approaches, you will need to check what policies and processes are in place at your own institution, and in your department.

PERSONAL TUTORING AT YOUR INSTITUTION

Below is a list of questions you should ask (there should be some written guidelines for staff and students, but you may also need to ask colleagues about some of these questions):

- Are students normally allocated a personal tutor for the duration of their degree, or do year tutors take on some aspects of this role?
- How many students are personal tutors usually responsible for?
- How is this usually reflected in workload allocations?
- Is the emphasis primarily on the student's academic progress, or do tutors undertake a more general pastoral role?
- How are students given information on what to expect?
- Are there any discrepancies between the written guidelines and what happens in practice?
- Is someone in your department designated as a mentor or adviser to new tutors? If not, make a list of colleagues you might approach for advice or support.

You should also get hold of a list of the specialist support services offered by the university, and keep it for reference. See 'Specialist advice and referrals' on p. 58.

Once you have a clearer idea of the broad context for your position as personal tutor, the rest of this chapter will focus on helping you to improve your own effectiveness in the role.

FIRST MEETINGS

New students will usually be allocated a personal tutor at the start of their course, so plan for an introductory meeting as soon as you receive your list of new tutorial students.

Ideally, this first session should be programmed into induction week for all tutorial groups. However, if there is not a standard system in your department for meeting new tutees, try to arrange to see them briefly as a group during induction week. This is a good way to introduce yourself and to set the scene for future meetings.

If there is enough time, try to structure the discussion to help the group explore any questions and anxieties they may have. For instance:

- You could ask the students to talk in pairs for a few minutes about their expectations of the course, and together make a list of any questions about the course or starting university. Pairs can join up into small groups to compare their lists, followed by the group as a whole sharing ideas on how to resolve any common issues. This reassures them that they aren't alone in their concerns, and that their fellow students can be a source of support and encouragement.
- You could also encourage them to recall previous experiences of transitions (such as going to secondary school) and the kinds of strategies that were most successful in helping them to settle in.
- Answer any direct questions about the course, but remember they may already be feeling overwhelmed with information at this stage, so don't overdo it.
- *The Student Induction Handbook* (Bourner and Barlow, 1991) includes several other ideas for working with first-year groups to help them find out about the course and each other. Some of the questions suggested below for a first individual tutorial could also be adapted for a group session.

If a group tutorial cannot be scheduled, then send a welcome note to each one of your tutees, introducing yourself and inviting them to come and see you individually. Give details of where and when they can find you, whether you offer regular 'drop-in' sessions and how they should sign up for an appointment.

47

QUESTIONS FOR THE FIRST TUTORIAL

The first tutorial meeting is important to help establish a comfortable working relationship. Sue Wheeler and Jan Birtle (1993) suggest some open-ended questions as basic starting points for a first tutorial:

- Tell me something about yourself.
- How do you feel about being here?
- How does the college differ from your school?
- What do you expect from your experience here?
- What kind of extra-curricular activities do you hope to become involved with?
- Is there anything that you are anxious about with respect to being a student?
- What personal resources do you have that might help you to settle in here and enjoy yourself?
- Have you thought about what kind of career you would like to follow?

(Wheeler and Birtle, 1993)

It is useful for you and the student to discuss and agree any points for future action, and to note these down. Check whether your university has systems in place for recording tutorials (and see also the section on written records later in this guide).

At this stage it is worth clarifying any tutorial ground rules, especially about confidentiality, and reminding the student of the overall purposes of the tutorial system. The student should be aware that you are not just here to help with problems, but to offer support for their overall academic and personal development.

PERSONAL DEVELOPMENT PLANNING (PDP)

All university students in the UK are now expected to engage in a process known as personal development planning (PDP). PDP operates alongside the student's other subject-based learning and accompanies it, offering opportunities for organisation, focus, direction and reflection, all of which enable the student to plan their personal development and know what they have achieved and what they still need, or want, to achieve. It aims to enable students to own their own learning and develop the necessary skills and personal self-confidence in their skills that will help them as people and employees in the future.

In general, the benefits of PDP are that it encourages students to take more responsibility for themselves and their own development. This should foster a more proactive and mature approach to academic work, reducing support needs and making tutorials more purposeful and enjoyable. It also helps students to make connections between their course and life beyond the university.

There are some systems in place in universities where students might be assigned to a Student Services colleague or student adviser to help them to become involved in, and further, their PDP. In many instances this support is part of the role, so their personal tutor has the most frequent support relationship with the student, whether they have difficulties in university life and study or not. When it is part of the tutoring role it might well be seen as a natural everyday interaction and not an activity that seeks to redress a deficit or sort out problems. It is certainly not intended to be seen as a deficit activity. The most successful self-aware students are likely to be the most involved in developing their PDP profiles or portfolios, while all students can benefit from the organisation, the cohesion and development involved in undertaking a portfolio or progress file. This process offers them development and clarity about their skills and achievements, which enables them in composing a CV (curriculum vitae) for a job, or presenting themselves to an employer who wants to know what kind of skills they have developed while they have been studying (not just what subject, because that's clear from the degree – to a point). Historically students might well have kept a written file of their work and development. Indeed, in FE and school the progress file accompanied the student through their studies and went with them to employment or further study after completion. PDP for HE students serves this need. In some instances, PDP can also be developed online, where students reflect on their work and complete certain development tasks to clarify skills needs and enhance their record of achievements over time. In these instances they can locate their portfolio or progress file in an online location rather than on paper.

Encouragement from staff is an important success factor, so it is helpful if you mention PDP and invite students to bring relevant materials or reflections to tutorials. However, they also need to understand that ownership and responsibility for their personal development as a whole belongs with them.

PERSONAL DEVELOPMENT PLAN (PDP) AUDIT

The development of a PDP often begins with a skills audit in the context of the wider range of skills and personal qualities needed to be a successful student and a successful historian, accountant or other professional job role towards which the student is heading. Often, following the audit, plans for development are drawn up and it is then part of the tutorial meetings or special PDP meetings – or online activity – that the skills development and learning development are revised regularly. A pre-arranged agenda can form part of regular tutorial meetings at each stage, dependent on the course structure. For instance, following on from the suggested topics for a first meeting, a scheduled review towards the end of Level or Year 1 might include discussion of coursework results, and using feedback from module assignments to help the student identify areas for development. Later meetings might focus on such topics as module choices, preparation for placements, dissertation subjects and career plans.

If students keep the same tutor throughout their degree, then your final meeting might be used to agree a summary of their achievements and qualities, based on the evidence they have been gathering for their PDP. This could then be kept on file for use when answering future reference requests.

STUDENTS WITH DISABILITIES

It is particularly important for students with disabilities to meet their personal tutor at an early stage, to explore any support needs or necessary adjustments to teaching or assessment strategies, and provide a sound basis for regular progress reviews. However, don't assume that all students with disabilities will necessarily have problems. Most will have effective strategies in place before they enter HE, and will simply require a reasonable level of flexibility and good communication with their tutors (see Chapter 7).

WRITTEN RECORDS AND CONFIDENTIALITY

It is helpful to take a few minutes at the end of any tutorial to review what has been discussed and confirm any actions that have been agreed. For example, a student might be encouraged to focus on improving their essay-writing skills, or to keep a diary for a week to help with time management.

Encourage students to keep their own written notes of the summary and agreed action points. This helps them to take ownership of any decisions and to act on them, rather than perpetuating a more passive 'parent/child' relationship in which you are expected to sort out any problems for them.

Your university may also have a system for formally recording tutorials, with a copy for the student and another for the student file in the School office. However, any recording system also raises the question of confidentiality – how confidential are personal tutorials expected to be? It is important that students feel they can trust you enough to talk freely, but it is equally necessary to be clear about any limitations on this.

The need for clarity around information about disability was discussed in the previous section. Similar principles should apply to any other information disclosed in tutorials (e.g. about domestic problems, or bereavement). If it might affect the student's ability to fulfil the demands of their course, encourage them to let relevant staff know about it or ask if they would like you to do this on their behalf, but don't do so without explicit permission. Whatever is agreed about disclosure to staff, you should, of course, never discuss information from individual tutorials with other students.

Be aware of any procedures for submitting a 'mitigating circumstances' appeal if a student's performance is adversely affected by circumstances beyond their control, such as serious illness or bereavement.

You should not feel obliged to keep confidential any information that might compromise your own position (for instance, if a student is telling you about a serious breach of the law) and should make this clear if such a situation arises.

The other time when confidentiality may be over-ridden is where there is a genuine concern for the student's safety (for instance, where they have expressed suicidal feelings) requiring notification of their GP or other specialist help.

PRACTICAL ARRANGEMENTS

It is important to make ground rules explicit. If students need to talk freely about confidential matters, they will want to know whether they have five minutes or half an hour, and that they won't be overheard. If you share an office with colleagues, you might need to find somewhere else to hold tutorials. In your own room, you could use a sign on the door to deter interruptions.

Some institutions have introduced policies to restrict one-to-one meetings, to avoid accusations of harassment on either side. Otherwise, common sense should guide you, but if you do have any concerns about meeting rooms or other arrangements for tutorials, discuss them with colleagues to help you identify practical solutions. For instance, you could keep the door open, use a teaching room or one with a glass panel rather than a small, enclosed office, or arrange for a colleague to be nearby.

ARRANGING REGULAR APPOINTMENTS

In most universities, students are entitled to a scheduled meeting with their personal tutor to review their academic progress on a regular basis. Who is responsible for arranging these meetings?

 ACTIVITY

What would you do if a student on your list:

■ Has not made an appointment to see you for several months?
■ Has not responded to a direct invitation to see you?
■ Has been giving course tutors cause for concern, e.g. by poor attendance or failing coursework?

Discuss your responses with colleagues. Could improvements be built in to the current system in your school?

Although there are arguments in favour of encouraging students to take the initiative themselves, the disadvantage is that those in greatest need of support or review might fall through the net.

Particularly in the early stages of the course, it is important to schedule meetings for all students and to follow up any non-attendance. Research into retention has shown that an early appointment for an informal discussion about how students are settling in will help them make the transition to university more effectively and identify any issues/concerns before these reach crisis point.

Another advantage of setting a fixed time for subsequent tutorials or periodic progress reviews is that both tutor and student can prepare in advance. You can ensure you have copies of the student's assessment results, etc., and the student can be encouraged to identify recent successes and areas for improvement, to help focus the discussion.

Most programmes will have key times in the year when many students are facing common issues, such as examination nerves, and it may be worth arranging an extra group tutorial rather than dealing with queries on an individual basis.

 ACTIVITY

- What would be the most suitable times in your course for two regular meetings per academic year?
- What topics might be raised at each stage of the course?
- Are there any key points in the academic cycle where a group tutorial session could help students address common issues?
- Are there any arrangements for encouraging students' own self-help or tutorial support groups (TSGs)? (See Chapter 9 for some suggestions on helping students to run their own support groups.)

UNSCHEDULED MEETINGS

Whatever the policy on scheduled meetings, most students will also wish to see you at other times. Some tutors put tutorial timetables on their doors for students to sign up to, while others run 'drop-in' sessions at specified times.

 ACTIVITY

- Find out what is the usual system in your department, and the average length of time allocated for meetings.
- How do students know how to make an appointment?
- How easy is it to contact you from outside the university (especially important for those who are part-time, disabled or live some distance away)?
- Can students telephone your office, or do you prefer email? Giving students your home telephone number is not usually recommended, although some staff do so in special circumstances, such as for research supervision students.
- Could any aspect of the appointment system be improved?

Many new tutors start by trying to be accessible at all times, but then feel overwhelmed by constant interruptions and demands. It is useful to explore these issues in advance.

ACTIVITY

- What do you feel about saying 'Not now' when someone says they need to see you urgently without an appointment?
- How can you tell when it is a real emergency?
- Do students feel they can only come to you if they have a problem?

There are no simple answers here, but it is worth thinking through the advantages and disadvantages of a completely 'Open Door' policy, on the one hand, or a very rigid appointment system on the other. A key concern is the need to ensure that students feel cared for as individuals without undermining their autonomy and sense of personal responsibility (or, indeed, your own entitlement to a realistic and manageable workload).

ACTIVITY

- Discuss these questions with some of your colleagues.
- Look again at your responses to the questions about Expectations (p. 45). How do those answers relate to the issues raised here?

LISTENING AND OTHER TUTORIAL SKILLS

Two of the most important skills needed for tutorials are listening and questioning. Most tutors and counsellors recommend using open-ended questions to initiate discussion; for instance, 'How are you finding the different aspects of the course?' might be more productive than 'Is everything OK?', to which the student might feel obliged to answer 'yes' and no more. Unless the student is obviously distressed, it is also useful to spend a few minutes together setting an informal agenda for the meeting – ask them what the key points are that they would like to cover, or use a standard format (e.g. progress since the last meeting, recent highlights, issues and queries, agreed action points).

It's equally important to allow students enough time to explore for themselves the issues that are raised, whether academic or personal, and to develop their own ideas about what to do. A real difficulty for personal tutors is to see oneself primarily as a source of information and advice. If so, you might be tempted to jump in too soon and just tell the student how you think they should act. Try to avoid being too directive – instead, attend closely to words and body language, and hold back your own comments or questions until they have had time to say what is on their mind.

After the student has finished speaking, you could reflect back what you think they have said, to reassure them that you have been listening attentively and to enable them to correct any misunderstandings. Asking one or two questions can open up the discussion and help them clarify the underlying issues. For instance:

- How do you feel about what is happening?
- What are the options for you?
- Tell me more about . . .
- What would need to happen to make you feel better about . . .?
- What would you like to change?

These questions are adapted from Wheeler and Birtle, *A Handbook for Personal Tutors*, Chapter 3 'Counselling and Listening Skills'. The chapter as a whole is full of practical examples and discussion of case studies and dilemmas.

NOTES AND ACTION POINTS

Towards the end of the discussion, it can be helpful to agree jointly some realistic action points and, if appropriate, a time for a further meeting to follow up on progress.

Always try to allow a few minutes soon after any tutorial to make a quick note for yourself about how the session went and any ideas on how this could have been improved. This will help develop your awareness of tutorial dynamics, which is particularly helpful where there are few external role models. You will probably have observed a wide range of teaching styles in lectures and seminars, but your knowledge of personal tutorials may be limited to your own experience as a student, usually with a single tutor.

It might be possible, with permission from the student concerned, to sit in on a colleague's tutorial, or ask a colleague to observe one of yours, to broaden your experience and help you identify the kinds of tutorial contributions that seem most effective.

You could also record one of your own tutorials, again with permission, so you can review it later and see where you might have handled things differently. For obvious reasons, a scheduled session is likely to be more appropriate for this than a crisis meeting.

Another good way to explore different approaches to tutoring is for a group of colleagues to discuss anonymous case studies, which can bring out surprisingly different attitudes as well as allowing you to benefit from other people's experience.

COMMON CONCERNS

Apart from improving your tutorial 'technique', it is helpful to think about the kinds of issues that students are likely to present. These fall into a number of basic categories.

Problems with academic work might include:

- *Worries about course choice.* It is very common for new students to wonder if they are on the right course. This might be related to other anxieties and will be overcome as they gradually settle down generally, and you can help them best by enabling them to deal with the kinds of concerns outlined below. However, in some cases, it might be necessary for them to review their course choice. Careers Advisers can be very helpful here in offering unbiased advice and a chance to talk through the issues (see Specialist advice and referrals, p. 58).
- *Difficulties with particular modules.* Try to encourage them to discuss this with the module leader first; if they are reluctant to do so for any reason, talk through the issues with them, but avoid inviting criticism of professional colleagues. Instead, help them to identify the underlying problem (e.g. inappropriate module choice, specific academic difficulty, personality clash with staff or students . . .) and possible solutions for themselves, as this will help them to cope better in the future.
- *Difficulties with general academic skills, such as writing essays or coping with examinations.* Apart from offering direct advice,

you could encourage students to attend any study support services offered by your university.

- *Dyslexia or other specific learning difficulty.* If you suspect this is the case, encourage the student to contact Student Services for an expert assessment.
- *Time management.* This is another common problem, particularly during the first year. Students who have been used to reminders from parents or teachers at every stage of A-level coursework can find it hard to manage multiple deadlines on their own. Help them to draw up a sensible work-plan at the beginning of every term, but avoid taking on a 'parental' role or nagging them about this – they need to learn how to take responsibility for themselves.
- *Difficulties with other students.* This often arises from group projects, which can easily spark personality conflicts. Avoid taking sides, but help them to work towards a compromise. As with other transferable skills, the ability to work well in groups requires practice and some support.

 ACTIVITY

- Make notes on other academic problems that might arise, and think ahead about the kinds of support that would be most appropriate.
- Check with colleagues to ensure that you know where to access relevant information and resources.
- Keep a note of recurrent issues, and consider building appropriate 'study skills' support into first-year modules, or running free-standing sessions with other tutors.

Financial difficulties

These are increasingly common and can have a cumulative effect on students' work, with stress and anxiety often combining with too many hours of part-time employment to cause academic under-achievement or failure.

Apart from just offering a sympathetic ear, encourage them to think about whether they could reduce some kinds of spending – many first-year students really do find it hard to get a balance between study and fun at first. A gentle reminder that they should consider switching to a part-time registration if they really must work in excess of recommended maximum hours for full-time students, can help to focus priorities.

However, students in more serious difficulties should be referred to Student Services or the Students' Union for relevant advice and possible assistance. Most offer financial advice and specialist advice on welfare benefits and debt counselling.

Personal problems

If you have built up a good relationship, it is quite natural that students will see you as their first port of call if they have any personal problems, but be aware of the professional support offered by central departments and other specialist agencies. Although you should expect to give advice on academic matters, do *not* attempt to take on the role of a personal counsellor.

When a student comes to you with a serious medical, financial or other personal problem, listen sensitively to what they are telling you, but avoid the temptation to offer well intentioned but amateur advice. Use open questions to help the student clarify the issues in their own mind, and encourage them to make contact with Student Services, who will refer them to an appropriate specialist if necessary.

See the section below on Specialist advice and referrals and keep contact details easily available for reference in tutorials.

SPECIALIST ADVICE AND REFERRALS

You can usually contact your Student Services department for advice on referring students for specialist support. Counselling services may also help you to talk through difficult tutorial events and help you look at strategies for possible future situations. The following advice is based on Counselling Services guidelines for dealing with particularly difficult or disruptive situations:

- If someone is very upset or angry, try to stay calm yourself. Let the person finish what they are saying so you can understand what it is they want. Ask them calmly to explain the bits you don't understand. Keep judgements to yourself.
- Acknowledge the person's emotion directly, e.g. 'I can see how upset/angry you are and I would like to try and help you'.

- Do not get angry yourself – their anger is not personal to you but will be an accumulation of events and pressures.
- If the student is very upset, offering them a cup of tea or coffee will also give you time to decide the best way forward. Tell them about the services that you feel might help them and offer your telephone for them to make an appointment.
- Ask the student to let you know if they got the help they needed – show your interest in helping them resolve their difficulties.
- If you don't have time to deal with the situation then it is better to say so, e.g.: 'I understand what you want but I'm due in a meeting shortly and I want to make sure I give you the time you need – what time can you come back this afternoon?'
- Ask the student if there is anything else he or she wants from you.
- If you don't know how to help be honest about that, e.g.: 'I understand what you want but I'm not sure who can provide that for you. Can you give me some time to make some calls to establish where you can get the help you need? I will keep your personal details confidential.'

REFERRING A STUDENT ON

It is worth thinking carefully about how to introduce the suggestion that the student might speak to someone other than yourself. It is important that they don't feel you are just trying to offload them and their problems, but that you are genuinely concerned to ensure that they get the most appropriate support. Listen carefully before suggesting that a particular issue may be outside your own area of expertise and then do whatever you can to help them to make an appointment with someone who can help – usually the relevant member of Student Services.

It is usually best not to make this initial contact on the student's behalf, and certainly not without their permission. Counselling services suggest that in 80 per cent of cases where someone else has made the appointment, the student will fail to attend. However, if you are worried that they might avoid seeking the necessary professional help, and the matter seems urgent, offer the appropriate contact details and let them use your telephone during your meeting so they can make initial contact immediately. If that is not possible, then give them the information they need, in writing, to enable them to do so later.

Do not expect to receive any feedback about the outcome of a referral. Other professionals are bound by confidentiality rules just as you are. However, check that the student is aware of this, in case they are anxious about it. Alternatively, they might prefer you to know what is happening and automatically assume that you will be kept up to date by other people. Ask them to let you know how they get on and to come back to you if there are any problems or delays. This will reassure them that you are not trying to ignore their difficulties, but are genuinely concerned to make sure they get the appropriate support from a qualified professional.

It is worth familiarising yourself with the areas covered by Student Services (information on the CLT website – see 'Useful websites' below) and also discussing with colleagues the boundaries between your own role and that of Student Services staff. Any group of staff could use fictional case studies such as those included on the CLT website, or other hypothetical or anonymous examples, to explore responses to the general issues and to discuss when a specialist referral might be the most appropriate action.

 ## FURTHER READING

Bourner, T. and Barlow, J. (1991). *The Student Induction Handbook*. London: Kogan Page.

Earwaker, J. (1992). *Helping and Supporting Students*. Oxford: SRHE/Oxford University Press.

Fry, H. and Kettering, J. (eds) (1999). *A Handbook for Teaching and Learning in HE*. London: Kogan Page.

Jaques, D. (1989). *Personal Tutoring*. Oxford: OCSD.

O'Connor, K. M. and Oates, L. (1999). *Academic Tutoring*. Special No. 11. Birmingham: SEDA.

Thomas, L. and Hixenbaugh, P. (eds) (2006). *Personal Tutoring in Higher Education*. London: Trentham Books.

Wallace, J. (2000). 'Supporting and guiding students'. In H. Fry, S. Ketteridge and S. Marshall (eds) *A Handbook for Teaching and Learning in Higher Education: Enhancing academic practice*. London: Kogan Page.

Wheeler, S. and Birtle, J. (1993). *Handbook for Personal Tutors*. Buckingham: Open University Press.

USEFUL WEBSITES

The CLT website : http://staffcentral.brighton.ac.uk/clt/resources/personal_tutor.htm. This has a section on personal tutoring as well as copies of case studies for departmental discussion and other relevant resources and links.

Chapter 4

Mentoring, work-based and community placement support

Mentoring is a work-related development activity with individuals and so resembles the kind of supportive engagement you might also have with students who are developing their skills in work-related activities, and in community-based placements. We will look first at mentoring and then consider the other two more briefly, since the same skills are likely to be used in each of these contexts.

This chapter considers two kinds of mentoring that could support students in a variety of contexts:

- mentoring – as a form of development between professional or academic mentor and students;
- peer mentoring, when students mentor each other.

Mentoring – as a form of development between professional or academic mentor and students – is often used in the development of work-related skills, professional behaviour and role completion. The role for the mentor is to both support the mentee through their development into the professional role or their further development in a work-based setting, and, in many ways, to model, as well as reflect on and explain, the ways in which the role of professional behaviour evidences best practice.

Since mentoring is both a peer process and one that is hierarchically constructed (whether this is admitted to or not), the mentor is chosen for their experience in the professional work-related tasks or role and the mentee is chosen, or chooses, to work with the mentor in order to develop their skills and expand their experiences and insights. It is not a role you would normally adopt as a teacher with an undergraduate unless they were work shadowing and learning how to develop as a professional. If you are a discipline-oriented professional: an architect, a social worker, a teacher or a nurse, for example, this kind of mentoring might be part of your work with students.

ACADEMICS MENTORING STUDENTS

Much mentoring between tutors, other academics and students is seen as a support or even remedial exercise. As a system, it often is built to support new systems, troubled ones, and those on work placements, although the James Cook University example (discussed later in the chapter) and several others indicate that it can be used more generally for the specific development of work-related skills, in placements, and to support learning more generally.

Some of the literature focuses on the experience of the mentor but most studies of the effectiveness of the system in practice are in relation to mentees, and consider descriptions and evaluations of the commonality among aims, structures, strategies and processes of implementing and then evaluating mentoring in action.

In a comprehensive survey of the literature on mentoring in the context of young people, Gulam and Zulfiqar note the characteristics of mentoring as: 'conceptually it is the classic strategy: the more experienced shall care for and train the less experienced, in a non-judgmental manner' (Gulam and Zulfiqar, 1998, quoted in Hall, 2003).

The emphasis on 'care' and a 'non-judgmental manner' distinguish mentoring from other forms of instruction. However, Philip (1999) comments on terms associated with mentoring:

> Mentoring can hold a range of meanings and the terminology reveals a diverse set of underlying assumptions. For example, youth mentoring has been associated with programmes aiming at coaching, counselling, teaching, tutoring, volunteering, role modelling, proctoring, and advising. Similarly the role of the mentor has been described as role model, champion, leader, guide, adviser, counsellor, volunteer, coach, sponsor, protector, and preceptor. A similar range of terms may apply to the mentee, protégé, client, apprentice, aspirant, pupil, etc. The process itself may also be described variously as 'reciprocal', 'helping', 'advising', 'leading', or 'facilitating' as 'a collaborative enterprise' with shared ideals or as a 'learning process' by which the mentor leads by example. In general however knowledge and understanding about the processes which take place within mentoring relationships remains at a preliminary stage.
>
> (Philip, 1999)

This is a little confusing. Roberts (2000), in a re-reading of mentoring literature published between 1978 and 1999, identifies the essential characteristics of mentoring, defining it as having:

> the essential attributes of: a supportive relationship; a helping process; a teaching-learning process; a reflective process; a career development process; a formalised process; and a role constructed by and for a mentor. The contingent attributes of the mentoring phenomenon appear as: coaching, sponsoring, role modelling, assessing and an informal process.
>
> (Roberts, 2000)

The mentor gains a great deal from the relationship with the mentee since both learn from each other. One of the key elements of mentoring is for the mentor to want to support and help the mentee develop and to share with them some of their own thoughts, practices and coping strategies. In the case of mentoring in education, this would most probably be learning strategies and those related to the student experience, but if it is a mentoring situation related to work, whether in the workplace itself or on placement for work-related projects, the mentor might well also be involved in modelling, and the mentee in shadowing their practice then discussing choices made and decisions taken.

If you act as a mentor to students or staff, you are both modelling and guiding them in their job role development to be more effective, and in their own interpretation of the kind of skills and knowledge with which you have worked with them. You will find you learn a lot from the reflection this causes you too.

MENTORING NEW STAFF

Alternatively, you might be called upon to be a mentor of a new member of staff in your role as a supervisor or teacher, and a postgraduate student might be called on to mentor an undergraduate or new postgraduate in terms of their work as a researcher, developing research skills, their teaching roles or other academic practices.

PEER MENTORING

Students often find that by entering HE or moving into another stage of their learning, for example, into work-based learning or the undertaking of a dissertation or other research project, they would benefit from the kind of close developmental relationship and modelling that mentoring between peers offers. At James Cook University in Queensland, Australia, a peer-mentoring process set up by Helen Treston from student learning support has been in operation for many years. The process here is that new students entering HE can use the services, expertise and support of a small group of mentors who are students who have been through at least one year of the university system already. These mentors are trained and supported by a staff member from Student Services and the study skills support team of the university. They, themselves, develop varieties of skills in the mentoring process, as do all mentors. They learn to match their teaching and learning behaviours against those of other kinds of learners, for example. The mentees might well be used to behaving differently from some of the mature or more established mentors as learners in terms of motivation, learning styles, approaches and outcomes. The mentors and mentees learn to consider the learning needs of others and the mentors learn to support and help those others in terms of their learning and personal issues in settling in and becoming a full member of the university's social as well as study culture. This helps the new students engage further with their subject at university.

MENTOR AND MENTEE TRAINING

The mentees have training sessions that help them determine their own learning needs and skills. They look at working with diversity, time management, dealing with difficult people, communication skills including listening, and develop a variety of skills that actually fit them well for the workplace after graduation. In developing any form of peer mentoring it is important that the mentor community and individuals are made aware of the skills development they are gaining themselves, so that they gain confidence and can market their skills with employers after graduation. Many of those mentored on this scheme go on to be mentors themselves, as the mutuality of this support is empowering for the mentors as it is enabling for the mentees.

SETTING UP MENTORING GROUPS

You might help identify and seek interest among the students who have been at university for over a year to see if they would like to form a small mentoring group who will receive developmental training and be focused and organised to work with the newer students or those with particular learning needs, whether these be issues of ability and disability or second language learning. Mentors could be trained in time management and communication skills, including:

- listening;
- basic counselling referral strategies for those who need counselling;
- working in small groups;
- information sharing on the key functions and people in the university who will work to support students in their learning;
- information acquisition and retrieval;
- study skills;
- how to work one-to-one with others in a semi teaching/coaching capacity;
- dealing with difficult people;
- working with diversity;
- student learning behaviours, styles and approaches;
- how to work with different learning behaviours and needs.

Bringing mentors together to work with them as a community will support them in their learning and their own sense of identity as students, as we can help them develop useful employability skills and to complete their own PDP and CV.

At James Cook University, for example, the mentors are a group of dedicated and visible individuals who work with any student who can benefit. They have training, T-shirts to identify them, special use of library space to see mentees and computer use for themselves, and a yearly trip to the Great Barrier Reef! (not all universities can offer that sort of incentive, but there could be less exotic others). Building a community of mentors clearly enhances the job prospects through acquisition of transferable skills for the mentors themselves, so the benefits go beyond a kindly response to support others.

PEER MENTORING

Mentoring is also something students do with each other. Worley and Martin (2005) described a scheme, in St Mary's in 2001, which aimed to use peer mentoring to enhance the quality of each others' writing. They argue that good analytical writing is nurtured in a social environment.

In response to this they stimulated a social environment with peer mentoring and the beginning of a peer tutoring project. They were convinced that the more students were willing and able to look at each other's writing, the more that writing would improve. They brought students together to critique each others' work and tutors were asked to begin sessions by asking students what concerns they had about their writing, then to respond to this. They

> were impressed by the quality of student responses to written work, and when they exchanged work with each other, the tutors, too, saw the value of the peer review process. Their satisfaction levels with their own writing increased, as did their enthusiasm for discussing writing challenges with other students. In subsequent years, when we increased the period of training from two to ten hours, we concentrated less extensively upon lecture sessions and more intensively upon the practical work of reviewing student essays.
>
> (Worley and Martin, 2005: 4)

Despite difficulties, these systems clearly worked in enhancing the skills of students as writers. Dinitz (2004) assessed this project and reported that the programme

> benefits both student clients and student tutors . . . Students' comments often revealed that the tutor addressed both higher and lower order concerns; for example, one student mentioned learning how to use commas and getting good ideas for the conclusion. In their comments, the tutors reported having learned a lot about writing, having become more self-confident about their abilities in general, and being very satisfied by the experience of helping their fellow student.
>
> (Dinitz, 2004: 3)

As with most examples of mentoring, the experience was mutually beneficial.

Hall's (2003) work on mentoring considers large-scale US studies and both the ill-defined nature of the term and the unproven claims for its success. But he does explore the US literature that has identified a number of key features that help to make successful mentoring schemes. These include:

- monitoring of program implementation;
- screening of prospective mentors;

- matching of mentors and youth on relevant criteria;
- both pre-match and on-going training;
- supervision;
- support for mentors;
- structured activities for mentors and youth;
- parental support and involvement;
- frequency of contact and length of relationship.

In considering the UK literature, he notes that mentoring needs to be properly integrated into its organisational context and to establish appropriate links with other services and opportunities, so that those being mentored have a fully rounded experience that goes beyond this one-to-one work.

WHAT CAN GO WRONG?

Although there are debates about how to match up mentors and mentees, there seems to be agreement that mentoring can be unsuccessful if there is:

- social distance and mismatch between the values of mentor and mentee;
- inexpert or untrained mentors;
- mismatch between the aims of the mentoring scheme and the needs of the person being mentored;
- conflict of roles such that it is not clear whether the mentor is to act on behalf of the person being mentored or of 'authority'.

This last issue looks at the political role of the mentor, which is a concern for many who write about the role, i.e. that it is possible a mentor is working to ensure compliance, training mentees in acceptable behaviours rather then problematising and critique.

BENEFITS

Mentees value and benefit from their relationship with their mentor, and who the mentor is *is* an influence in this process. It is important that values are matched and the research tells us that most mentors are female, so nurturing skills might well be being deployed. Mentors tend to be female,

67

white and middle class. There are many benefits for mentors being part
of mentoring schemes and these are:

- having a role and identity in the university;
- gaining satisfaction supporting the work of others;
- self-esteem;
- social insight;
- social and interpersonal skills.

(adapted from Hall, 2003)

ONLINE MENTORING

Mentoring can be conducted face-to-face and also online. Supportive comments and information exchanging can be most useful at a distance (see
Chapter 8) as nurturing and structured relationship building is well suited
to the controlled yet caring and sensitive interaction possible online.

Kent (2002) ran a pilot project in which online mentoring was offered
to black and Asian students and graduates. While traditional mentoring is
both very resource-intensive and often difficult to arrange due to time
constraints, online mentoring, it is argued, can potentially accommodate
work with many more graduates and students than traditional face-to-face
mentoring. It can also help to overcome time and distance barriers. Band
and Parker (2002) also focused on ethnic minority students where cultural
distance and difference that might present a barrier face-to-face is largely
irrelevant in an online environment.

Characteristics of successful mentoring include:

- development of skills;
- increased confidence in both mentee and mentor.

SUPPORT FOR STUDENTS FROM DISADVANTAGED
BACKGROUNDS

Mentoring and PAL are often used as successful strategies to support the
learning of students of more traditionally disadvantaged backgrounds in
all contexts and, particularly, in some cultures, such as that in South Africa,
where increased access to tertiary education has, since 1994, systematically
transformed institutions until they better represent the demographic
profile of the country. This means that previously disadvantaged groups
of students (defined as black, coloured, female, handicapped, Indian,
mixed ancestry) are studying, and many need further support, being the

first generation undertaking a university career. Page *et al.* (2005) focus on the experience of the University of Stellenbosch over a six-year period and the development of a uniquely African tutor/mentor system that services both students shown to be at risk of failing and those who are gifted but underachieving, in a most successful manner.

SUPPORTING STUDENTS ON COMMUNITY PLACEMENTS

Community placements for students have been common in US universities since the 1980s and are now increasingly popular within the UK. Community placements are seen as valuable not only for student learning, but also for enhancing the effectiveness of local organisations and the lives of local people, and for strengthening the university's relationship with its local area. Students benefit from the opportunity to:

- relate their academic work to real-life situations;
- develop their work-related skills;
- improve their communication skills and confidence;
- contribute to projects that 'make a difference';
- gain a more holistic university experience.

The process of preparing and supporting students for community placements is, in many ways, similar to preparing and supporting students for work-based learning. However, students on community placements may need specific training and support to develop social and community awareness and to work with a wide range of people, including 'vulnerable people', such as those with mental health issues, learning disabilities or people who have survived trauma or abuse.

Community placements can take place as part of wider courses or as specific courses and modules on 'learning in the community'. In either case, there must be a clear structure for both students and staff to work within. Students can identify for themselves a placement or be allocated one. They will, ideally, attend several preparatory sessions within the university before going into the community. The community organisation may require students to undergo Criminal Records Bureau (CRB) checks before starting their placement, which may add extra time to the preparation stage. Once in their placement, students must complete a set number of placement hours, e.g. twenty, thirty, or fifty and must keep a reflective journal of their experience. An academic tutor – usually the module leader

69

– will meet regularly with students, e.g. fortnightly or monthly, to assess their progress and to discuss any difficulties. A community-based mentor is desirable, however this may not always be possible within the placement setting. Requiring the student to submit regular written assignments is another way of assessing their progress and is also a means of rewarding and accrediting students' participation. Assignment tasks can range from providing a reflective account of practice, to undertaking a literature review, writing a case study of the organisation, or undertaking and evaluating a particular activity within the placement. Students could also be encouraged to produce a CV, documenting the skills acquired during the placement.

Tutors involved in organising and assessing community placements need to bear in mind that they have a dual role – to assist the learning of the student and to contribute to the effectiveness and wellbeing of the community organisation. Tutors must hold structured discussions with a key representative from each placement setting to ensure that both parties are fully aware of one another's values, priorities and expectations, and that they agree on how the placement will operate and how the student will be supported. A contract should be produced between the organisation and the university, setting out the terms of the placement and the responsibilities of each side. Ideally, the student will also sign this contract – this may be in addition to a learning contract the student must sign for the course. Tutors involved in organising community placements should, themselves, feel confident in the role. Tutors will probably have community-based experience themselves, will teach and research on community-related issues, or will have access to information, training and support to ensure success in their new role.

SUPPORTING STUDENTS ON WORK-BASED LEARNING PLACEMENTS

Since the Dearing Report emphasised 'employability' in 1997, work-based learning (WBL) has become increasingly central to university courses. WBL is defined as learning undertaken for, at, or through work. Learning is usually accredited though a university-based course – this could be a Foundation course or a traditional undergraduate degree. The Quality Assurance Agency (QAA) (2001) states that, on an undergraduate course, students need to develop skills in four key areas: Interpersonal; Information Handling; Drawing Conclusions; and Personal Development. WBL plays an important role in achieving these learning aims.

As with community-based learning, the WBL placement is a partnership between the university and the external organisation or employer and the university must take care to understand the expectations of the employer and ensure sensitivity to their needs. Students must be encouraged to understand and be supported to see themselves as 'employee' rather than 'student on placement', and to adhere to the employer's work-based practices, whether or not they are paid for their work. However, they also need to understand the requirements of their academic course, and how they will be assessed and accredited for their placement. A learning contract is a good idea – reviewed and renewed at key points during the placement or the year.

Students on WBL placements should have two advisers – one based in the organisation (often called 'the mentor') and one based at the university ('the supervisor'). The role of the supervisor is to advise and facilitate learning, and particularly to guide the student through the various assessment tasks involved, e.g. developing a portfolio, keeping a reflective log, evaluating personal learning. Meanwhile, the mentor is responsible for guiding the student through the work-based tasks and the development of particular work-based skills.

Onyx (2001) suggests that academics, as WBL supervisors, must combine their traditional role with a more 'hands-off' approach: the academic supervisor is somewhat distanced from the learning and has the role of observing, monitoring and assessing student learning rather than directly facilitating it. Part of the supervisor's task is largely administrative rather than teaching. They must identify the placement or help the student to do so; arrange contracts; structure inductions; monitor progress and assess learning. The roles of 'Assessor' and 'Manager of the Learning Process' are the two key elements of the supervisor role, Onyx states.

Boud (2001) provides advice for organising supervisor–student contact time during WBL placements, to ensure maximum benefit from the limited time available. He identifies various stages in the WBL process that can provide structure for supervisor–student meetings. These stages include: the learning agreement negotiation stage; the orientation phase; and the assessment stage. Boud suggests that supervisors can provide learning resources and train students how to use them, to make the most efficient use of time. This then allows supervisor–student meetings to focus on those issues that really must be discussed one-to-one and which cannot be handled any other way, e.g. helping students to understand assessment requirements and helping students access university resources.

One of the most important benefits of WBL, and a key role of the academic supervisor, is to help students become self-directed with their learning. Brockett and Hiemstra (1991) offer a checklist of ways that facilitators of learning can promote self-directed learning. These include: helping students to assess their individual needs and map out their own path; pointing students to resources and showing them how they can be accessed; promoting a positive attitude to self-directed learning; asking questions and encouraging the student to solve their own problems (see also Chapter 2). The academic supervisor needs to recognise the skills needed to support WBL and build a strategy for developing these skills into their professional plan.

FURTHER READING

Band, S. and Parker, A. (2002). *Ethnic Minority Undergraduate Scheme (EMUS): Post mentoring research*. London: National Mentoring Consortium, University of East London. Available from: www.uel.ac.uk/nmc/mentoring/index.htm. Accessed 25 September 2007.

Bierema, L. and Hill, J. (2005). 'Virtual mentoring and HRD'. *Advances in Developing Human Resources*, 7 (4): 556–68.

Boud, D. (2001). 'Creating a work-based curriculum'. In D. Boud and N. Solomon (eds) *Work-based Learning: A new higher education?* (pp. 44–58). Buckingham: SRHE/Open University Press.

Brockett, R. and Hiemstra, R. (1991). *Self-direction in Adult Learning: Perspectives on theory, research and practice*. London and New York: Routledge.

Brown, G. (2004). *How Students Learn*. London: RoutledgeFalmer.

Capstick, S. (2004). 'Benefits and shortcomings of peer-assisted learning (PAL) in higher education: an appraisal by students'. Paper prepared for the Peer Assisted Learning Conference at Bournemouth University, January 2004. Available from: www.peerlearning.ac.uk/pal_conference_2004.html. (Revised versions of these conference papers may have been published since.)

Cropper, A. (2000). 'Mentoring as an inclusive device for the excluded: black students' experience of a mentoring scheme'. *Social Work Education*, 19 (6): 597–607.

Dinitz, S. (2004). 'Assessment of "Exploring the Potential of Peer Tutoring in Developing Student Writing" project'. Higher Education Academy English Subject Centre. Available from: www.english.heacademy.ac.uk/archive/projects/reports/peertut4_mary.doc. Accessed 25 September 2007.

Gulam, W. A. and Zulfiqar, M. (1998). 'Mentoring: Dr. Plum's elixir and the alchemist's stone'. *Mentoring & Tutoring*, 5 (3): 39–45.

Hall, J. (2002). 'Mentoring and young people: a literature review'. *SCRE Research Report 114*. Available from: www.scre.ac.uk/resreport/pdf/114.pdf. Accessed 25 September 2007.

—— (2003). *Mentoring and Young People: A literature review*. Glasgow: University of Glasgow.

Kent, M. (2002). 'Online mentoring – a role in widening participation?' *Learning and Teaching in Action*, Issue 1. Centre for Learning and Teaching, Manchester Metropolitan University. Available from: www.celt.mmu. ac.uk/ltia/issue1/kent.shtml. Accessed 25 September 2007.

Onyx, J. (2001). 'Implementing work-based learning for the first time'. In D. Boud and N. Solomon (eds) *Work-based Learning: A new higher education?* (pp. 126–40). Buckingham: SRHE/Open University Press.

Page, B. J., Loots, A. and du Toit, D. F. (2005). 'Perspectives on a South African tutor/mentor program: the Stellenbosch University experience'. *Mentoring and Tutoring: Partnership in Learning*. 13 (1): 5–21.

Parsloe, E. (1995). *Coaching, Mentoring and Assessing: A practical guide to developing competence*. London: Kogan Page.

Philip, K. (1999). *Young People and Mentoring: A literature review for the Joseph Rowntree Foundation*. Aberdeen: University of Aberdeen.

Quality Assurance Agency (QAA) (2001). 'The Framework for Higher Education Qualifications in England, Wales and Northern Ireland', January. Available from: www.qaa.ac.uk/academicinfrastructure/FHEQ/SCQF/2001/. Accessed 2 November 2007.

Roberts, A. (2000). 'Mentoring revisited: a phenomenological reading of the literature'. *Mentoring & Tutoring*, 8 (2): 145–70.

Wallace, J. (2004). 'Retention, an intended outcome'. Paper prepared for the Peer Assisted Learning Conference at Bournemouth University, January 2004.

Wheeler, S. and Birtle, J. (1993). *Handbook for Personal Tutors*. Buckingham: Open University Press.

Whittaker, M. and Cartwright, A. (1997a). *The Mentoring Manual*. Hampshire: The Gower Publishing Company.

Worley, J. and Martin, M. (2005). 'Writing in the dark: bringing students' writing into the light through peer tutoring. A final report on the project: "Exploring the potential of peer tutoring in developing student writing"'. HEA English Subject Centre newsletter, no. 9. Available from: www.english.heacademy. ac.uk/archive/publications/newsletters/newsletter9.pdf. Accessed February 2008.

USEFUL WEBSITES

Bournemouth University. Peer assisted learning: www.pal.bournemouth.ac.uk.

Mentoring and tutoring: www.tandf.co.uk/journals/titles/13611267.asp.

Chapter 5

Supervising projects and dissertations

This chapter considers some of the strategies and practices you could use to supervise undergraduate projects and dissertations. This is probably the first large-scale piece of relatively independent work students have done and their first real chance to engage in a learning conversation with an individual tutor, you, as the supervisor. This is both a human interaction and one that requires the engagement with, and development of, research skills. It is crucial that you get on together professionally, so clarifying and using your interpersonal skills is one important element to be aware of. It is also crucial that the student learns to own the project themselves and to develop the appropriate research and writing-up skills that will enable them to carry out future research projects. So, this is both a personal/ interpersonal activity and one focused on developing skills and completing a project. Students will expect you to know about the systems and practices of the university, rules about length of work and hand-in dates, and to guide them as to their participation in any introduction to dissertation development.

START WITH THE LEARNER

It's always a good idea to start by considering what your students' expectations might be, how they could be feeling about and planning towards this new area of work, and to find out and negotiate with them a manageable course of action that steers between the institutional and departmental requirements of the dissertation or project, and the students' own learning approaches, styles, behaviours and background. They might be feeling:

- excited – a chance to carry out a piece of research and work in an area they have chosen themselves;
- confused – not sure what to work on yet and in need of some guidance to select a manageable topic that enthuses them;
- overwhelmed – this is a huge piece of work;
- over-confident about how to do the work – perhaps seeing it as just gathering a lot of information and writing a lot of words – rather than asking questions and dealing with the ideas and arguments of others in order to develop their own ideas and arguments, then expressing them.

Some of this you can determine by talking with students about what they want to work on, what kind of work they have done before, and their experience with any kind of research, e.g. for an essay or project in the last couple of years at work, in school, or at college. Also, you can find out what kinds of skills they feel they might need to carry out the process, what is a realistic amount of time to spend on it, and how they normally go about their learning.

Their learning practices might vary from reading a lot to reading very little, gathering lots of notes then working out what to do with them, to asking a question and gathering information to help answer it. How are they able to meet deadlines usually? What do they know about the deadlines and demands of this project?

There will be departmental and institutional guidance on the size, shape, length and layout of dissertations, of projects that they need to consult – and which you could provide them with or send them to collect and read and use. There are also some useful books about getting started with a research project, and carrying it on through to writing up and completion – some students work well from such study advice books and others work better through discussion, or seeing and talking about examples, and/or trying it all out in stages then reflecting.

You will become more aware of how to work with your individual learner student over time, but it's a good idea to have some sense of their expectations, the demands of the discipline and the department for this project, and the kind of learning styles and behaviours they have been used to which might well need to develop somewhat for success in this new, longer project. Help them to make it real and see it as exciting and manageable.

MAKING THE RESEARCH AND DISSERTATION MANAGEABLE

For undergraduates, this is the longest piece of work they have been involved in and it is often quite daunting for them to even start. Preece notes: 'one common reaction is that the students become overwhelmed, not to say mentally paralysed, by the seemingly daunting prospect of writing so many words' (1994: 210). With that in mind one of the best ways you can help them overcome this and get on with a dissertation or project that is likely to pass, is to encourage students to be aware that they are:

- carrying out a piece of research;
- writing a dissertation;
- doing lots of other things – some of them predictable and other less so.

So, they need to plan for all three:

1   Developing a short realistic plan of the dissertation or project report helps focus the final shape, so the student can work towards producing parts of it looking at the shape required – abstract, introduction, literature review/theoretical perspectives, methodology and methods, chapters containing data and analysis and discussion of this, conclusions, references.

2   Planning the research and writing – using time planning and management – identifying what stages of the dissertation should be developed, collecting and analysing data, writing being drafted and rewritten, and the process edited, tidied up, finished off and presented – in time. A time plan from the start of the research process to the end, including writing right from the beginning, will help make this more manageable and realistic.

3   Drawing up a very brief time plan or critical path analysis, which shows where and when they think they can carry out various bits of the research, write up bits, and carry on with the rest of their work and lives. Doing this together makes it more real, and then you can each refer to it later when you meet for supervisions.

77

STAGES OF RESEARCH AND WRITING THE PROJECT OR DISSERTATION

Essentially, we probably need to match the stages of our supervision to the stages of the students' need to develop their research through to completion and their research skills for this and future projects.

1 Getting going and nuts and bolts

Processes:

- working with your student in identifying a fascination and topic and turning it into a research question;
- developing a conceptual framework or the ideas that will help hold the project/dissertation together;
- boundaries – areas they will not be researching and gaps – identifying what has been discovered and written about and what has not yet been asked or investigated, however specific this might be;
- developing a proposal for the project or dissertation;
- identifying the main theorists and theories and reading that will underpin and engage with the work;
- choosing methodologies, methods and research vehicles appropriate to the research topic that will help them ask their research question.

Organisation issues and practices are about managing the work and the time:

- learning contracts;
- agendas;
- ground rules;
- time and work management.

2 Starting the research for the project or dissertation
There are many skills that match the development stages of a report of a project or a dissertation. It is useful to discuss these with your student, auditing the skills they have already and working with them in identifying any research skills, needs and the opportunities for learning which aim to help them to develop these necessary skills. Some of these skills might include:

- time management – so that they can plan the project stages, work out how long, for example, data gathering and analysis will take, and how to stage their writing bit by bit, their editing and final referencing and production of the report or dissertation;
- learning about methods and how to put them into action with the research population;
- information gathering and managing the information acquired through the research process;
- analysing reading and deciding what information, arguments, themes and theories to use from reading to underpin the research and writing;
- keeping good notes, filing, cataloguing and ordering the research data;
- engaging in a dialogue with theorists and experts;
- processing data;
- writing descriptively, analytically, in an argument, using theory, developing a conceptual level to the discussion in the writing.

3 Maintaining momentum

In the middle period of any research project, however long or short, there are issues and problems that could arise and might undercut the research process or prevent the student's development of research skills and completion of the project.

Some of these potential difficulties might be about access to subjects, data, or hardware. Some might be about difficulties with processing, analysing, synthesising, organising, expressing, or about managing time and people, or managing data. Some other issues might be about managing life around the project itself. It is important to work out with the student what issues might be arising that could hamper their progress and, where possible, work with them to help them overcome these issues so that they might further develop their research through to completion. At this stage, it might be necessary to access Student Services or study support.

Some of the issues might be about their personal situation and the way that you are working together.

Handling interactions if they start to deteriorate: These require people skills:

- getting on well with your student;
- dealing with difficulties;

- working with learning differences;
- encouraging students to make learning leaps and respond conceptually, as their work continues;
- supporting, encouraging and continuing to guide, empower and model for students so that they develop research skills further;
- supporting their analysis of their data;
- overcoming various possible hitches such as losing their sample, finding their hypothesis has no grounds, becoming bored with their subject;
- encouraging students to write as they go along and edit.

4 Completing

Towards the end of the project students need to engage with stages of interpreting their data and developing findings, writing up their work in the appropriate shape for assessment. They are involved in the stages of:

- analysing and interpreting data;
- turning it into findings and conclusions;
- writing up and editing, testing it out with a critical friend, with their supervisor, rewriting and editing until the work is as well expressed and as well organised as possible.

5 Presentation

In the final stages of the project report or dissertation students are involved with ensuring appropriate presentation. They need to think about:

- rules of presentation;
- layouts of tables, data, artefacts and text;
- ensuring appropriate referencing, abstract and shape to the whole project.

As you look through these different stages you might find it useful to consider the interpersonal skills of supervising, the particular stages of the student's research, and the representing or presentation of that research.

SUPERVISOR ROLES

Supervisors work with both the learning development towards completion of the project and, to some extent, the personal development of the student.

There are probably a few roles we might feel more comfortable with, but it could be the case that very different learners working at different stages in their research will require different kinds of roles and responses from us, so it is useful to consider what these might be and how we might have to develop from our normal or preferred styles to cope with student and research-stage needs.

ROLE AUDIT

Which of these roles do you feel more comfortable in? When and why? (You might find it useful to pick more than one for different contexts.) They have been identified by supervisors in workshops in the UK, such as in the OU, London School of Hygiene and Tropical Medicine, and outside the UK in Griffith University and the University of the West Indies, among others.

Roles to consider:

- manager
- doctor
- mum/dad
- god/shaman
- facilitator
- mentor
- advocate
- counsellor
- friend.

Mostly the roles need to be balanced, and occasionally, if you do not seem to be making progress with your student and if they are getting stuck, however well you are getting on with them, you will need to diagnose whether you are using the right version of the role to actively help them develop, become rigorous and imaginative, and to act with independent judgement and develop their own voice in the writing.

If you become too friendly, act as their mum/dad or friend, then you might get too close to the student to be able to make constructively critical comments. However, they will need the kind of nurturing into independence that those roles suggest.

If you end up counselling them about personal issues, you might not be able to focus on the work, and the counsellor's job is best carried out by experts (see Chapter 3 on personal tutoring and referral). Although the student might think you have all the right answers and are, for some reason, withholding them, and although you are indeed in an authority position, however friendly you are, you are neither a god (omniscience!) nor a shaman (with magical powers!). It is important that they realise you are advising them, not telling them what to do and providing the final right answers. Research is a learning journey, it goes in several new directions before it settles into a project that can be completed and written coherently.

ESTABLISHING GROUND RULES AND CONTRACTS

Good supervisions have to run over a fairly long period of time – for undergraduates this is usually up to a full year, and for postgraduates (see Chapters 10 and 11) it is much longer. With this in mind, it is very useful to learn from the kinds of self-regulation that colleagues involved in independent learning have stressed (Boud, 1995). Developing a learning contract is one such element that aims to help students and supervisors determine a way of working together, timescales and behaviours that can enable the student to complete the project, and the supervisor to support them in this completion. Learning contracts have been used on the independent learning degree at the University of East London (UEL) by David and Carole Baume, and with a variety of students at the University of Technology, Sydney (among other contexts).

A learning contract can be as formal or informal as you decide between you, but it does provide the opportunity to sit down together and decide what working rules, behaviours and agreements can support you in your ongoing supervisory relationship.

Some questions to consider in developing a learning contract

Answering these questions might help you to define and agree a learning contract between you, which will help to structure both the student's work and the working relationships between you over time:

- What do you want to achieve?
- How often should you meet?
- Who should do what in advance of each meeting?
- What work should be done between meetings?
- What skills need developing?

- What does the supervisor agree to do (read in advance, pass information and reading to the students, help inform and develop students' research skills and their writing and so on)?
- What does the student agree to do?

You might draw up the answers to these questions into a contract where the supervisor agrees certain behaviours and expectations and the student others – just to clarify your preferred and manageable ways of working.

Some common agreed ways of behaving

At an early meeting it is good to agree elements of a learning contract, formal or informal, deciding on boundaries and expectations such as:

- when and how your student can contact you, with short questions or with work to consider;
- how long you will take to get back to them;
- sending you work in advance of meetings that you will comment on in advance;
- discussing the work at the meeting with each having developed a few questions in advance;
- taking notes and action points and agreeing actions in a time frame.

The student could be asked to:

- develop a timeline and a needs list ready to undertake the research;
- send writing in advance of meetings, and email with small requests and problems;
- stay in touch.

You are not the only one who can work with your student. Look at Chapter 9 on helping students to help themselves and work together. They might find it useful to share their work with a larger group for critique and developmental suggestions, and/or to work with another student in your group and share work in progress and make critical (constructive) comments for clarity and coherence.

Fellow students could:

- work together to write an abstract;
- test out writing with each other – is it clear?;
- consider whether the claim made (argument, claim for the meaning and findings of the work) is backed up by evidence.

Other students are a valuable resource to augment your own support.

IF THINGS GO WRONG

Things can go wrong with your student's research project or dissertation, and things can go wrong between the two of you in terms of your student/supervisor relationship.

Let us look at the two separately, although they are certainly related, i.e. if you are not getting on well together or your student is avoiding you because their work is somewhat blocked – then the work will suffer.

Lucinda Becker, in *How to Manage Your Arts Humanities and Social Science Degree* (2003: 26), recognises that things go wrong particularly at the end stage of the research and writing up. If students can identify and work through a problem with a tutor who then helps them plan future work strategies, they are better able to take responsibility for the rest of the work. Expectations of you as a supervisor are high though, since supervisors as the first point of contact seem to be expected to know exactly what to do to help the student out of the difficulty.

Identified difficulties

Problems students identify with supervisory arrangements include:

- unclear tasks;
- unclear boundaries;
- not being able to learn from feedback;
- not being able to contact the supervisor when difficulties arise;
- the supervisor does not actually know exactly what to do to help the student get over the problem, i.e. there is little skill in personal or study strategies and little knowledge about the workings of the institution.

84

You cannot be expected to have all the answers. Some of the ways of tackling problems that arise rely on person skills, others on your skills as a researcher and in other cases, or perhaps you need to advise the student that they should turn to others such as counsellors or Student Services. You also need to know about departmental rules and regulations, about extensions and so on. Part of your role is knowing the rules and enabling the students to get on with the work and the writing up. The better organised you are with your work with your students, the clearer the ground rules, boundaries and roles, and the better your knowledge about the processes of research and writing and the rules and regulations of the university, the better able you are to enable the student to get on with the work themselves and to develop the kind of research skills and autonomous working skills that they will need in the future. Most universities run courses for supervisors of postgraduate students and many have courses for supervisors more generally. It is worth accessing one of these courses or seeking a mentor yourself as you start to supervise for the first time, so that you are well prepared and the role can be creative, developmental and successful.

FURTHER READING

Baume, D. (2003). *Managing Environments for Portfolio-based Reflective Learning (MEPRL) – Goal sharpening*. Newcastle: University of Newcastle. Available at: www.eportfolios.ac.uk. Accessed February 2008.

Becker, L. (2003). *How to Manage Your Arts, Humanities and Social Science Degree*. London: Palgrave.

Bell, J. (1999). *Carrying Out Your Research Project*. Buckingham: SHRE/Open University Press.

Boud, D. (1995). *Enhancing Learning Through Self-Assessment*. London: Kogan Page.

Preece, R. (1994). *Starting Research*. New York: Martin's Press, Inc.

Walliman, N. (2001). *Your Research Project: A step by step guide for the first time researcher*. Thousand Oaks, CA: Sage.

Wisker, G. (2005). *The Good Supervisor*. Basingstoke: Palgrave Macmillan.

—— (2001, 2nd edn 2007). *The Postgraduate Research Handbook*. Basingstoke: Palgrave Macmillan.

Chapter 6

Dealing with diversity 1

This first diversity chapter will focus on different kinds of learners in relation to learning approaches and styles, and will then concentrate on some issues and practices related to working with international students.

The second diversity chapter (Chapter 7) looks particularly at academic advising and work with students with disabilities, including those who have mental health issues. Both chapters rely on the background in how students learn and in academic advice including referral.

The student body has changed a great deal over the last twenty or so years in response to a widening participation agenda and a desire to see a higher proportion of young people, in particular, accessing HE. Additionally, mature student numbers have been maintained. One consequence of this is that we are now working with diverse students. If, historically, HE was seen as a rather elite experience accessed by both the socially and educationally or intellectually elite, now its aims include all those who have the ability, potential and motivation to benefit from its opportunities and support. In our several roles working with students we are likely to meet a variety of expectations and needs from this diversity of students, for some of which we might need to seek support from Student Services, and other specialist elements of the university in order to deal effectively with issues that emerge, and with the diverse needs of the diverse student body. It is important not to feel inadequate in ourselves – the other services are in a partnership with us. We need to ensure that students seek and make good use of the services they offer, but we also can be useful and helpful in the first instance as study advisers and enablers of student learning.

Some of the issues students present relate to learning styles and approaches, some others to their origins, their diversity in relation to age, gender, educational background and experience, sexuality, religion, and how these affect their learning approaches and engagement, and some to their abilities, disabilities or mental health issues. This chapter considers diversity in student learning in terms of learning styles, approaches and backgrounds, and takes international students as a special case. Chapter 7 continues this focus and considers the role for study adviser, and supporting the learning of students with disabilities particularly those with mental health issues.

DIFFERENCES

The students we supervise, mentor, coach, tutor or work with in one-to-one sessions are likely to represent a wide range of differences in terms of their learning backgrounds or approaches; the conceptualisation of what knowledge is (epistemology); their sense of what reality is; how they can relate to reality, information, knowledge and learning in the world and so how they can set about working with their subject at undergraduate or postgraduate level. Some of these students represent variations in study approaches, background and context in relation to their origins, perhaps being the first in the family to undertake university study; coming from a family where English is a second or third language, or having learned in an international context where learning was a different experience to what is expected in the UK. Some might have physical or other disabilities that affect their ease of learning in the ways that suit the majority of students. Differences include:

- age
- gender
- ethnicity
- origin
- economic status
- religion
- ability
- physical and mental ability or disability, including mental health.

Some of these differences are obvious in meeting each other and others do not immediately emerge in your work together. For example, students with mental health problems are often unlikely to mention this on any official forms. In the case of dyslexia, however, it is more often stated on forms, diagnosed and tested, and so incurs support and perhaps an allowance for them to work on checking their spelling and construction.

DEALING WITH DIFFERENT KINDS OF LEARNERS

We all learn differently, although those who research student learning approaches and styles have worked on defining categories, patterns and underpinning theories that help to clarify the similarities and differences. It is possible for those of us who try, to take such differences into consideration as far as we can when working without students. It is always difficult to teach to some of the hidden diversity in the lecture theatre and seminar room, because unless students present as physically quite different, thus suggesting they might have culturally affected learning styles or learning needs, we cannot actually see that we have such a diversity of learners with us. However, working one-to-one with students in a supervisory, personal tutoring or other relationship, provides a very special opportunity to experience interactions with individual learners. What we learn about their learning and how to work with, support, nurture and empower them as learners, is never lost in the future as we return again to the large lecture theatre or new group, aware that we have before us a visible or hidden diversity. What might be causing these differences and what might they be like? And how might we as supervisors/tutors and as lecturers take these differences into consideration in all our teaching and support?

LEARNING STYLES AND APPROACHES

At the beginning of the book, in the first chapter, we looked briefly at deep and surface learning (Brown, 2004; Entwistle and Ramsden, 1983) and there are a wide range of other learning theories that go some way to explore and categorise rather than explain student learning approach and style differences. This whole approach has been criticised in so far as it is often unproven, does not scientifically categorise students and their learning approach styles, behaviours and ways in which they might learn or work, make the best of their learning styles and approaches and extend these farther to benefit further. However, human learning is not a precise science. How could it be? If you believe that we construct meaning, interpret and make meaning from events and experiences rather than there being fixed meanings and fixed facts, and if you recognise human subjects as shifting, changing, becoming, able to learn and grow, affected by context, environment and the demands and modes of learning, then it is no surprise that any theory about student learning will be questionable because human beings are not scientific models and not measurable in experiments and trials. They are varied and any learning situation is always varied. We attempt to keep some elements stable in order to provide equality of opportunity and quality of experience. This chapter does not mean equality of access to something fixed, but instead diversity on offer and response to enable a fair and just experience. It means altering how we offer the curriculum and the student experience so a wide variety of students have access to it.

So it is with diversity of learning styles. It is also important to remember that students' learning styles (defined as ways they learn effectively – seen as tendencies but actually varying over time) and approaches (the ways in which they approach their learning, make sense of it, act, based on styles and context and demands) and their learning behaviours (what they actually do when learning) will be affected by:

- age;
- gender;
- ethnicity;
- culture;
- context;
- discipline;
- learning environment;
- the rest of their student experience;
- learning background;
- previous formal and informal learning experiences;
- the demand of the task;
- the context of the learning (individual, group seminar, lecture, work-based, etc.);
- learning outcomes;
- the cues of the learning – what is expected, the way you introduce and model tasks and outcomes.

All of this is in play in relation to their origins and learning abilities, disabilities or learning needs. There is no logical reason why a housebound student confined to a wheelchair should be better able to learn remotely one-to-one using a computer, nor that an able-bodied, sports-playing, white, Anglo Saxon, middle-class male should be better able to learn in the kinds of groups in which he socialises and plays his sports – it is a varied mix.

STUDENTS LEARN DIFFERENTLY – CUES

Graham Gibbs talks of interviewing students about their learning styles and approaches. One student, asked about their learning on a particular course, talked of a response that was largely characterised by surface learning, i.e. memorising, behaving quite mechanically in response to orders, collecting facts and repeating them back in assignments.

One student talked about the independent learning, the flexibility and imagination he used in learning and how he was involved in the transfer to experience and transfer of learning beyond the course he was studying. The 'punch line' is that these responses come from the same student – i.e. this student has been able to morph and modify his learning behaviours in relation to his perception of the expectation and demand of the course, the tutor, the context. Students learn how to learn, all the time. This learning about their learning, known as metacognition (Flavell, 1979), can really enhance that versatility.

Another anecdote: teenagers insist that they cannot learn from a rather chaotic, lively teacher. She does not organise their work for them; the notes are oral not written; the course does not seem to be following a rigorous and ordered manner; she engages them in discussion and role play rather than note taking. This is group work and interactive learning, but the students are used to something far more organised and angled. Their learning styles and approaches are at odds with each other. As a tutor you might be faced with such convergence or divergence. One of the issues here is the clear cues we give students – what are we expecting from them as learners? How might we give clear cues about:

- learning outcomes;
- criteria;
- learning approaches and behaviours?

WHAT CAN WE DO?

My own thoughts here are that:

1   As tutors and teachers we need to be flexible enough to change our teaching styles to suit the demands of the context, discipline, environment, learning outcomes.

But that:

2   We need to explore and explain and take our students with us
    on learning journeys, enabling them to be aware of themselves
    as learners who will develop their ability to learn in different
    ways so they can develop to change and fit new situations – and
    this might involve exposing them to learning activity they are
    not used to.

Explaining why the learning situations are constructed, and the activities
are taking place as they are, is a good first step to involving students in
diversity of learning.

Let us look at learner diversity according to various theories to consider
the kinds of learners we might be dealing with in our one-to-one situations, and then we can consider how we might work with this diversity,
encouraging students to be aware of themselves as needing to learn
differently in different situations and to adapt to both different learning
demands and different tutors.

HOW DO STUDENTS LEARN?

Very little is actually known about how students learn, and even less about
how research students learn, but some of the theories and vehicles for
finding out about student learning can help students and their tutors/
mentors/supervisors/coaches to define their learning style, learning
conceptions and approaches, and help students to discuss with you, and
then work out, how to learn from a variety of learning and teaching opportunities, and to seek opportunities to develop the necessary skills for some
of what could be called their gaps and weaknesses.

It is important to enable students to:

■   audit their skills honestly;
■   see what needs to be developed;
■   see where their strengths lie and how to build on them;
■   see what weaknesses might be here and how to address these
    with a change of focus, skills development;
■   and to plan towards this.

Much has been written recently about informal learning as well as
formal learning and also about the importance of the whole student

experience, cultural, social and personal, in relation to achievement in learning (Knight and Yorke, 2003). It is with this in mind that you might start and continue a learning conversation with your student about learning from the full variety of opportunities in a focused manner, over time, being aware, developing the reflective skills to identify and move on with what has been learned from these opportunities. Opportunities include:

- experiences
- information sources
- events
- situations
- other people
- personal reflection
- formal and informal taught events.

Being aware of preferred learning styles and approaches and of areas of weakness can indicate to the student how they learn already and how they might both build on and enhance this, and also refocus to learn from people, documents and experiences from which they do not normally learn, and when they could adopt learning styles and approaches with which they are not familiar. It will help your students to adapt their learning style and to recognise some of the potential strengths and weaknesses or pitfalls in their learning style and approach with regard to certain kinds of problem-based learning, group work, field work, practical, one-to-one, independent, online work and research activities, for example.

STUDENT PROMPT ABOUT LEARNING

It is useful to ask yourself:

- Why you carry out your learning and research, that is, what motivates you (such as parental examples, a sense of duty, a sense of fulfilment).
- How you conceptualise your learning (such as seeing learning as gathering more knowledge about the world or enabling you to fit new understanding into a conceptual framework and link it to your experience).
- What kinds of learning and research approaches you take (such as accumulating information and data, relating ideas and information holistically, all together).

■   What sort of outcomes you seek (such as gaining status yourself, seeing the world differently, bringing about creative change).

See the Reflections on Learning Inventory (Meyer and Boulton-Lewis, 1997; discussed in relation to postgraduate learning in Meyer and Kiley, 1998; Wisker, 1999).

It is interesting to clarify these kinds of issues and practices for several reasons. Learning makes new and different demands upon learners and they might need to develop learning strategies to cope with this. If your student is an international student, culturally influenced learning expectations and behaviours might well differ in the university where you are working with them, from those back home. Increased awareness of current learning approaches and the demands on learning development can make students aware of the need to develop an appropriate variety of learning approaches and behaviours for the study tasks with which they are engaging – note taking, essay writing, discussing in small groups, independent work, placements and work-based learning, dissertations and so on. Research into student learning (Entwistle and Ramsden, 1983; Marton and Säljö, 1976; Ramsden, 1979) has suggested that students broadly prefer one or more of three approaches to their learning, but that in different situations they can emphasise different approaches. Very generally, these strategies comprise:

■   surface
■   deep
■   strategic.

LEARNING STYLES: DEEP, SURFACE AND STRATEGIC LEARNING

Established research into student learning identifies two main learning styles – deep and surface learning (Marton and Säljö, 1976; Ramsden, 1979). It is suggested that 'traditional teaching' which is about delivering information and is teacher centred, largely encourages surface learning, particularly in Science subjects, but that deep learning produces better results and longer-lasting learning for the students because it encourages them to develop the learning in relation to previous learning, to experience, and to the context. Later work added a third category, 'strategic' learning.

93

1   The surface or atomistic learner tends to see knowledge as
    fixed and their job as a learner is to acquire a number of facts.
    Tasks and objectives are seen as discrete, time is very
    important, and any personal relation to the work is considered
    unnecessary, inappropriate. This kind of student relies a great
    deal on learning through gathering information and then
    memorising because they are not pulling ideas and facts
    together into a whole, related to their already developed
    learning or concept 'maps'.

2   The deep or holistic learner searches for deeper meaning that
    goes beyond any specific task or single item of knowledge.
    They relate discrete information given to a general, already
    established learning or concept map, and fit new ideas and
    learning in with prior experience and prior learning. Their
    ideas and information relate to their experience and their
    learning becomes more whole, more theirs, more available to
    be used to help answer future and current questions and deal
    with problems.

3   The third category of learning is strategic learning. Students
    who are mainly strategic learners might be so because they just
    want to gain the qualification, pass the exam, complete this
    particular task. Strategic learning focuses on the end product,
    the marks, with the main aim being to pass. Students then tend
    to chase grades and only learn what looks necessary. This is
    useful for exams, perhaps, but there is no linking and little
    retention of the learning.

Discussing and exploring the way in which they approach their learning
with your student can help them focus on ways they might move towards
deeper learning. The same learning research suggests that the most effective learners actually combine deep and strategic learning often so that they
really understand and can use learning, and are focused on the tasks set.

LEARNING IN DIFFERENT DISCIPLINES

Different discipline areas, and different parts of discipline areas, might be
taught in a way that encourages either surface or deep learning, and assessment tasks can encourage surface learning, which suggests memorising
without understanding and rapid fading of that knowledge, or strategic
learning, which suggests focusing merely to pass the assessments, by

asking questions that seem to require repetition of information without problematising, exploring or relating information to tasks.

There is conflicting research on this issue of how flexible students are since Ramsden (1979) shows that students can change their learning strategies to suit tasks, while Thomas and Bain (1982) argue that students develop a certain learning style and do not change it.

Biggs and Rihn (1984) show that while students might show tendencies towards one of the three main styles of learning, deep, surface or strategic, it is both possible and desirable to encourage the development of deep learning approaches because these are, overall, the most successful learning approaches. Deep learning and processing involves meaningfulness in learning. You need to know and understand to learn deeply and this is the kind of learning that lasts. The question arises as to how we might encourage students to become deep learners.

A deep-learning strategy, based on wide reading, relating new knowledge to what is already known, and so on, results in better learning. 'Better' here means a complexity of outcomes (Biggs, 1978; Marton and Säljö, 1976); satisfaction with performance (Biggs, 1978, Ch. 6); self-rated performance in comparison with peers or examination results (Schmeck, 1988; Svensson, 1987; Thomas and Bain, 1982; Watkins and Hattie, 1981). Deep learning relates new learning to previous learning and understanding, enables the learner to develop their own way through their learning, to develop meaning, and to integrate that deep learning with work, and future learning tasks and outcomes. It does not fade, it is owned.

It is recognised that Science students more usually adopt a surface approach and that the Sciences tend to call for this, but research carried out by Svensson (1987) suggests that those who learn to adopt a deep approach gain better exam results in the end (or become better learners).

OWNING THE LEARNING – METACOGNITION

A useful learning activity to encourage in the student is the development of an awareness of how they are learning. These arguments show that learners who contextualise their learning relate it to themselves and their own world. They concentrate on how they are learning as well as what they are learning. They are higher achievers than those who are less aware of, or consider irrelevant, such consciousness and contextualisation. These other, surface learners, concentrate instead on the acquisition of fairly disparate facts and the achievement of discrete tasks and objectives. Metacognition (Flavell, 1979) identifies student understanding of how they learn so that they are now better able to determine situations from which they learn more easily, situations in which they have to change their preferred learning behaviours, and how to reflect on the learning they have achieved, and to transfer it to a variety of situations.

Students' approaches may differ at different times and in different learning situations, which may produce a diversity of learning cues.

It might be useful to discuss with your students how to audit their own kinds of learning approaches, their suitability for the learning experience and demands of the current situation and what kinds of learning development might be useful for future success; try engaging them with the following exercise.

 ACTIVITY

Things to ask your student to consider:

- What kind of learning approach(es) do you normally take (deep, surface or strategic, or a combination)?
- What approaches do you seem to be taking as you start this new activity of learning?
- Do you feel you might find it useful to develop some strategies now and, if so, how and why?
- What kind of learner are you?

OTHER KINDS OF LEARNERS AND LEARNING

There are other theories that suggest tendencies towards learning styles, and spotting these in yourself can help you understand why you find it difficult to learn from some situations and in some contexts and easier in others. When you have such knowledge about your own learning, you can choose to plan to your strengths and/or to work on your weaknesses and develop further the learning styles that are not the most obviously successful for you. You could ponder which of the following four main styles (activist, reflector, theorist or pragmatist) seem to suggest your kind of learning (see Honey and Mumford, 1986).

Please look at Honey and Mumford's definitions of learning styles. You might agree with the broad brush descriptors of learning styles, or not, but they can be useful to start students thinking about how they know they learn, when and where in what learning situations or how they seem to learn, and what kinds of ways, contexts, situations they learn least well in. If your student would like to complete their questionnaire and analyse results for a more 'accurate' picture, this is available in their book *Using Your Manual of Learning Styles* (Honey and Mumford, 1986). A major proviso here, though, is that the learning styles manual is based upon recognising occupational trends or norms so that, in many ways, it is about learning styles in relation to employment or preferred job roles. It could, therefore, be useful for either discussion about PDP or some other form of early career planning as well as focusing students on when they learn best and where they could work to enhance their learning. These developmental elements can be encouraged by a conversation about their learning after they have reflected on their styles as described and / or taken the questionnaire and analysed its results.

LEARNING STYLES – FOR YOUR STUDENT

Each style has its own strengths and weaknesses. There are no 'good' or 'bad' styles. Your major styles will tell you what strengths you have as a learner, which things make it easier for you to learn and what you might be less naturally successful in or might need to work harder to achieve in. For example, practical people tend to be high activists and pragmatists so studying Engineering, Nursing, or other forms of science might well suit them better, while Philosophy students and lawyers might well indicate that being a high theorist or reflector would more naturally suit them for their study and job. Everyone has to engage with theory, however, everyone has to put it into their own context, action, or words in arguing in an essay or project – so being a balanced all round learner is more beneficial given the range of study and assessment expectations now.

The greatest variety of learning opportunities are available to those who can, to some extent, operate in all styles, who are clear, when facing a new situation or a problem, which style is most effective for them, and are willing to find out ways of learning in situations and for outcomes that are expected of them but not their favoured style or approach.

ACTIVISTS

Activists learn best from new experiences, new challenges and the need for quick responses. They like to involve themselves in immediate experiences, are enthusiastic and responsive about anything new, they answer

ACTIVITY

Reflective audit of learning styles, approaches and behaviours to carry out with your student

There is much research into students' learning styles (the way they learn more comfortably and naturally) and their approaches and behaviour (the way they go about their learning). Some of the research can help prompt you to think about yourself as a learner, when, why and how you seem to learn best and what context situations and learning demands seem to suit you less well. Please look through the brief descriptions of learning styles (adapted from Honey and Mumford, 1998) and consider:

■ Which descriptions(s) of learning styles best fit you and your learning?
■ Are there any learning situations that you find you are naturally happier with?
■ How do they relate to learning style? (For example, if you are more of a theorist you might tend to read excessively before starting fieldwork or beginning to work out your ideas, manage information and start to write.)

Are there any learning styles you find you do not seem to be happy with and learning situations in which you feel you do not learn easily? (For example, do you like to get involved with activities but don't seem to find the time to do any of the background reading? Do you prefer to talk things through in a group but feel uncomfortable working on your own?)

If any difficulties do seem to be coming out of this audit, what might you do to strengthen your learning behaviour and approach to carry out this kind of learning more successfully?

---

questions immediately, they engage in active set tasks. However, they can tend to act first and consider the consequences later, to be bored with consolidation and implementation, with tasks that take longer, demand more reading and theorising. They learn least well from activities that require them to take a passive role or to spend much time reading and theorising before making decisions and acting.

REFLECTORS

Reflectors learn best from activities that allow them space to think carefully about, to reflect over experience and assimilate new information, new ideas, before making a decision about what they have learned, what to do, in their own time. They tend to be cautious and thoughtful. They want to consider all the possible angles and implications and to reflect back on what has happened and forward to what could happen before making a decision. They often spend a good deal of time listening, observing and thinking. Reflectors learn least well from activities that require rapid action, quick decisions with little time for planning.

THEORISTS

Theorists learn best from opportunities that allow them to integrate theories in with observations in the context of the required action or decision. They like to think problems through step by step, assimilating new information and experience into a tidy, rational scheme, underpinned by their analysis, and by theories. They are comfortable using theories and models to explain things to themselves and other people but less comfortable with quick decisions, actions that seem less well informed by careful processing, subjective opinion or creative thinking. They learn least well in situations that they are unable to research in depth.

PRAGMATISTS

Pragmatists learn best from activities with a clear practical value that allow ideas, theories and approaches to be tested in practical or real-life settings. They are probably down-to-earth people who like to get on with things but also to use what they have read and discussed in forming their decisions. They can be impatient with open-ended discussions that seem to be going nowhere and they learn least from situations where learning is not related to an immediate purpose, direction or action.

It might be useful to discuss this set of learning approaches and styles with your students or even to ask them to complete the Honey and Mumford inventory and then discuss their varied mix of styles and what this means for what they know they can learn from and how, and what gives them problems and how to overcome these. Use it as a tool to open up discussion of learning.

LEARNING FROM EXPERIENCE

You might discuss with your students whether, and how, they feel they learn from experience and in so doing use the work of Kolb (1984) and experiential learning. This can be useful for all students and particularly those whose maturity means they feel less comfortable with their academic background but have a great deal of experience of a work life, domestic, personal and professional kind to draw on, those who come to learning from professional practice, foundation students who are likely to be practical in orientation and less used to theory, and those who have learned in the standard academic fashion from books but have not yet thought about integrating this book learning, research information gathering, etc. in with any of their experiences, or who realise they will be expected to be more practical in their study than they had thought and are now putting theory into practice so need to consider how to learn from that experience in practice – whether they be medical students, teachers, nurses, engineers, lawyers – or students of a host of other subjects where they might theorise first and then go into a work-related or work-based learning experience.

EXPERIENTIAL LEARNING

Much of what we have thought about experiential learning derives essentially from an under-researched theory by Kolb (1984) (following Dewey, 1963). It might be under-researched, but in discussion with students and practitioners, it does seem to describe the learning cycle that relates directly to experience, so it is still useful as a way of introducing to learners the possibly new ideas of learning from experience and integrating that in with their more academic learning, or for recognising the value, when theorised and put into practice, of their range of experience already gained.

Kolb's definition of experiential learning is that it is 'the process whereby knowledge is created through the transformation of experience'. His diagram (see Figure 6.1) enables us to consider with our students how learners start from experience, move through stages of reflective observation and abstract conceptualisation, then move on to active experimentation, after which they move into a new learning cycle, incorporating the experience, reflection and abstract conceptualisation.

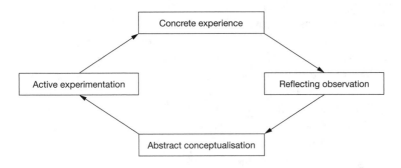

FIGURE 6.1   Continuous or experiential learning (after Kolb, 1984)

SOME QUESTIONS TO EXPLORE ABOUT LEARNING

How might you use experiential, continuous and other forms of learning theories and awareness in your one-to-one interactions with students?

Having developmental and learning-oriented discussions with students, which lead to their becoming more aware of themselves as learners; planning to learn in different ways; to reflect on their learning to engage it with experience and to move forward, all help embed learning and encourage students to own their learning. Other theorists add that deeper meaning develops with this use of continuous learning and if this can be added to with something creative, students move on to develop their own ideas, and some original work.

When reflected on, these activities can lead to self-reflection and personal transformation (Mezirow, 1985). The ideas of play and experiment (Gordon, 1961; Melamed, 1987), a creative release, exploration of ideas and practices can encourage students to use imagination and emotions, metaphors, games, simulations, creative modelling processes, in real field trips, projects, or virtual learning environments, in groups or individually. Being aware of the value of creativity and experimentation and encouraging students to think of moving beyond the assimilation and synthesis of knowledge is crucial for higher level learning at degree and postgraduate level. As supervisors or tutors you might help stimulate their creative energies by involving them in brainstorming or problem-solving activities, and also in considering how they might create something new beyond, and as a result of, what they are learning; in short, how they can engage their creative, experimental problem-solving, learning selves to make the ideas and learning their own and develop further.

There can be moments when students become more aware of themselves as learners as a result of all of these learning diversity activities, and this awareness leads to enhancement of their learning ownerships and what is called metacognition (Flavell, 1977). Through promoting discussion and feedback with students one-to-one, it is possible to nudge them forward into being self-aware learners. Some of these 'nudges' include the use of reflective diaries, portfolios, PDP and going carefully over written, or through oral, feedback prompting responses and learning decisions. These can all help in the development of metacognition.

REFLECTIVE PRACTICE

Reflective practice is another theory that integrates professional experience, reflection and learning. Donald Schön, in *The Reflective Practitioner* (1983), establishes a theory of how professionals and practitioners learn from experience. He argues that professionals respond to, and reflect on, the varied experience that arises in their work, seek development, learn, change, transfer what they have learned from one situation to another, bringing their past learning to bear on the new situation. Professional work and practice generate experience and knowledge naturally, and so can simulated professional or work-based experiences, field trips and work-based placements, but it is important to make this learning explicit in a learning situation, so as to encourage your student to reflect on and articulate their learning from practice and from their work (see Evans and Varma, 1990; Winter, 1995).

This is a useful reflective activity with all students, can be part of the beginning, middle or end of ongoing activities in the one-to-one discussion space, can form the basis of a PDP or just a conversation to focus students on their learning from experience. All these activities about student learning act to help students become more reflective, active, self-aware learners more likely to move on in their own learning. This is true for all kinds of learner including international students, mature students and those with mental health issues or with a variety of disabilities, whose learning we are considering next.

 **ACTIVITY**

An exercise to use with your student:

- What previous experience do you have in work, paid or unpaid?
- Thinking carefully, what skills, knowledge or attitudes/values do you think you have learned that could be transferred into or used in your studying here?

You might think of some specific skills or some more general skills such as: bench work, account balancing, analysis of documents, writing up reports, listening to others, managing your time, communicating in a variety of ways to a variety of audiences, everyday mathematics, dealing with diverse or difficult people, completing tasks in the times allotted.

- Are any of these useful in your study?
- What have you learned from your previous experience that can help you in your current study?
- What are you learning from the experience of studying?

These are general prompts to enable reflection and discussion and some further thoughts about building upon experience and learning from the experience of studying, integrating their learning and beginning to develop skills of metacognition.

INTERNATIONAL STUDENTS

International students are a large growth area for UK HE as they are for Australasian HE. For international students studying at a distance or away from home, there can be a range of issues of which the tutor/supervisor needs to be aware, from homesickness to culture change, to settling into new forms of learning.

A key issue when working with students from different cultural contexts is whether the approaches we have to learning, the suggested values and outcomes that underpin these, are themselves culture- and value-free or a product of a certain set of ideologies born of our own culture.

A norm in HE is to expect students from international contexts who choose to study with our universities to fit themselves into the learning culture and practices of the host university, effectively become enculturated, assimilated into its beliefs and practices. We need to ensure that in assuming this we are not insisting on research and student behaviours that are, themselves, culturally conditioned rather than good practice in themselves. Is our commitment to certain kinds of learning and research behaviour, for instance, merely a culturally inflected habit or approach? Might we be able to learn about different approaches and construction of knowledge from international students and so improve and vary our own practice and open up our thinking about how knowledge is produced, problems identified and addressed? What can these differing learning behaviours from different international origins and cultures afford? Or is it the case that international students might well want to learn the approaches and the boundaries of the host university and culture so that the degree they take back with them is definable by the country where they are doing it?

There are concerns that some international students tend to expect too much from staff, tutors and supervisors by way of guidance, support and even participation in their work to refine the language and expression. A related concern is that it is difficult to form relationships with some international students as colleagues and equals. The first step towards addressing these concerns is to understand the likely reasons behind them (Wisker, 2000).

> Many international research students come from higher education systems where it is normal to venerate age and experience and where it would be impolite to treat academics as anything other than near infallible. Consequently, when removed to a Western culture the students find it inconceivable even to consider entering into debate with supervisors. It would be impossibly rude to imply that supervisors' judgement could be anything other than perfect, and it would be arrogant to assert their own ideas and opinions. Their role, as they see it, is to follow whatever instructions their academic superiors choose to give them.
>
> (Okorocha, 1997)

Some cultures are so respectful of academic authority among other authorities that it would be rude of the student to engage in a debate with their tutor or supervisor, and similarly to engage in a debate with the theory of critics and experts, but we might argue that such a debate is the cornerstone of at least the British and also the Australasian education systems. It is important to raise such issues with the students so that they are aware of learning behaviours, interactions, expectations, the criteria, and relations and interactions with us, ranging between directive and eliciting, and the kinds of work expected from these interactions.

Students also need to become familiar themselves with language used in the disciplines, and with learning interactions in the discipline and between themselves and tutors, and other students, which are all potentially power-inflected issues. It is useful to make explicit such expectations about the shape of needs and processes regarding introductions, ground rules, boundaries, questioning and argument (a note about the word 'argument' – NB: engagement in critical debate does not mean 'attack' as some students think); respect for authorities but engagement in discussion with authority; developing your own voice and argument backed by evidence; and what exactly some of the strangely worded assignments really are expecting of students.

Clarification of a lot of these elements of the learning interaction as well as explanation for the kind of work expected in the:

- lecture
- seminar independent learning
- research
- field trips
- lab work
- project
- work-based learning placement

and so on, will better equip international students to engage with the system and its learning expectations of them. So, too, will clearly defined assignments and then backing up what is said in the theorised oral delivery with written words so that they can refer later on to the information and engage far more deeply with it.

ENGLISH

Many tutors mention the issue of students' written English as being a problem. It can be argued that there are at least three languages any student has to engage with;

- idiomatic everyday English in which we might deliver some of our information and general discussion;
- the language of the discipline;

- the kind of language academics speak which involves words such as 'discuss', 'doctorateness', 'critique' and so on.

International students are likely to come to us with facility in the middle version of English but be somewhat bemused by the everyday English and the instructions of describe, explore, discuss and so on which are used throughout the British educational system but do not quite mean what they seem to. These may need explaining and exemplifying to help students gain a grasp of what is intended especially in the world of assignments – modelling and examples are useful here.

Avoiding idiomatic expression in our explanations, or using them then translating into accessible English, this all can ease the student into the learning culture and stop the construction of unnecessary barriers.

LANGUAGE SUPPORT

Support for written language can be provided by specialist, subject-oriented language seminars. And the earlier in their programmes it is started the better, so many universities provide pre-study support, summer courses (University of Brighton) or international student access years (Anglia Ruskin University).

Articulating and sharing ideas, then work-in-progress, helps build students' confidence, contributing to the supportive community of peers. Shy or linguistically reserved international students need to be supported initially in their involvement in discussion. However, lack of such involvement is no indication that they find thinking and interpreting difficult, more that they are unused to voicing their opinions and hesitant in a new language context.

WHAT ELSE CAN WE DO?

Phillips (1987) reported that for seventy-six Indonesian students surveyed in the first year of Masters programmes at Australian universities, success was related not to language scores but to the kind and level of adjustments made by academic staff and departments to the students' needs. Similar issues are reported by other academics. Phillips pulls these together and notes:

The current situation is that small numbers of postgraduate students from a range of language and cultural backgrounds often study alongside native speakers of English accustomed to Australian teaching, learning and relational styles. Indeed, one reason for international students choosing to undertake postgraduate study in an English-speaking university such as those in the Australian system is often a desire to learn exactly these things, in order to facilitate later academic or commercial dealings. In this situation, adjustments to meet student needs clearly include appropriate provision of access to the existing academic, linguistic and cultural conventions of postgraduate study in the relevant discipline. Increasingly it is being realised that more is needed in the Australian context than the necessarily generalist courses designed to prepare students before their arrival, and that the most effective bridging may be that which is integrated into the early stages of candidature.

(Bartlett *et al.*, 1994)

Margaret Cargill (1996) reports on a successful US undergraduate 'adjunct' support model:

an ESL (English as a Second Language) course is linked with a selected content course and provides integrated language instruction using the course content and materials. This approach is being used at Murdoch University with first year undergraduates.

(Cargill, 1996)

Language skills or tertiary literacy are not the only indications of a student's level of understanding.

Most international students find 'receptive' language functions – reading and listening – easier than 'productive' ones – writing and speaking. However, the development of good oral communication is important if international students are to become full members of the department, participating in debate, problem solving and creative thinking.

(Okorocha, 1997)

Cultural reticence means that it can be argued that it is our responsibility to develop strategies for interaction with our students that enable them to learn, and practise how to use, the discourse of a subject and the kind of communicative language we use in discussion. Some students, particularly Asian women, tend to be quiet and retiring and need to be persistently involved, even if it takes a while for them to start to join the discussion, so that they have the benefit of airing ideas in exploratory talk. Giving them time to answer and using eliciting techniques that help them to explore the ideas are useful strategies.

There are widely held assumptions that many international students learn 'differently', i.e. rely on reproducing information and deference to, rather than argument with, authorities (Biggs, 1991). This is termed the 'myth of the Asian learner' and such deference to authority and reticence over engagement could pose a problem as engagement with arguments and debates are essential, especially for contextualised work and for research. Liz Todd (1996) considers that:

> Students often come from an environment where they are not allowed to criticise teachers, raise questions that could embarrass them or even to correct them if they make a mistake. It is therefore not surprising that they find it hard to put forward their own ideas. However, in the UK postgraduate students are required to demonstrate that they appreciate that other findings are not to be simply accepted and reproduced, and to show that they understand how knowledge in a certain discipline is constructed.
>
> (Todd, 1996)

Cultural inflections to the students' study need to be fully identified and taken into account. Comments on international undergraduates about culturally inflected learning differences and needs are equally true of postgraduates: 'There are many common sense reasons for arguing, and there is also emerging empirical evidence, that at least some aspects of students' conceptions of learning may be embedded in cultural (or even religious) beliefs and practices' (Kiley and Meyer, 1998: 8). See also Biggs (1991), Hughes and Wisker (1998), Samuelowicz (1987).

Developing supportive tutorial advisory and supervisory practices is essential in relation to (culturally inflected) learning styles and expectations without undermining their aims and outcomes, or adopting an unintentionally culturally imperialist stance with regards to their work. We need to ensure that suggestions of development of work are not merely products of a different cultural context.

Kisane Slaney, in her work with a group of international postgraduate students studying at Curtin, invited supervisors and students to work collaboratively on strategies to enhance students' English language skills at postgraduate level and set up action research sets – for supervisors and postgraduates to monitor and facilitate the development of these strategies and their usefulness in the students' own postgraduate research. The action research involved collaborative developmental work with the supervisors; regular supervision and joint sessions to enable idea exchange between supervisors and student; ongoing monitoring and final evaluative session in a collaborative mode 'to obtain a picture of the development/enhancement of the student and supervisors' communication skills, in the context of the supervisor relationship and the students' postgraduate studies' (Slaney, 1999: 73).

Slaney's summary of reflective questions for supervisors of students whose first language is not English provides a useful guide to all supervisors, tutors, etc.:

- Have I made my *expectations* explicit to my student?
- Have I seen the *totality* of my student, and taken into consideration the impact of her/his *life-world* upon his/her studies?
- Have I taken into consideration the possibility that my student will be going through a process of *transition*, as she/he negotiates cultural and disciplinary *border crossing*?
- Have I taken into consideration both my student's and my own need to work on *interpersonal communication*, addressing issues of *gender, race, ethnicity*, etc.?
- Do I have a process of *documentation* in place with my student, whereby we can record *actions, reflections* and *progress*?

Additionally, from our work with international students, we could ask:

- Does my student need to develop a range of research and support skills?
- These have not been necessary in their previous university or workplace, perhaps because they are unavailable, or because others have carried out the tasks for them so why do they need them now and how can we ensure they are given the opportunity to develop them?
- Can I spend some time inducting my students into appropriately polite behaviour to others in the university (including administrative staff) when seeking their help or just interacting in an everyday manner? Lack of politeness might be due to shyness, or the acceptability of different behaviour at home.

109

- Have I made time demands and deadlines sufficiently clear?
  In some cultures meeting times and work deadlines are less
  clearly defined, more flexible than the US/Australia/European
  context.
- Could I make contact with others in the student's culture or
  read up about it in order to be better aware of experiences,
  behaviours and norms? Could I call on these contacts if some
  difficulties in communication arise?

(adapted and added to from Slaney, 1999: 73)

Okorocha also has a series of suggestions ranging from orientation about
other cultures and cultural issues, examination of implicit assumptions,
showing interest in students' welfare, negotiating student/supervisor
etiquette and meaning clarification.

From whatever origins, cultural background and learning experience,
students each present a unique mixture of inflection such as age, learning
background, gender, sexuality, religion, culture, disability, language facility and skills. In focusing on any one student we will meet a kind of cross
hatching of these different issues so that an international student whose
cultural learning background has insisted on authority and respect for
the word of teachers might well be affected by their gender and age to
challenge such expectation (or not), and those whose culture expects
challenging oral engagement, and behaviours and single-sex classes might
find they are expected to engage in a big discussion with others of both
genders. Some students cultural background is disturbed if they come from
cultures where a female tutor is most unusual and they might find it difficult
working with one, so that their previous experience and these expectations
need respecting in our interactions with students, but not necessarily
reinforcing. They will need inducting into the variety of rich learning
experience from which they can benefit.

It is important to work with the needs and expectations of learners and
so to challenge, explore and facilitate their development and engagement
with the different expectations and opportunities of HE, while ensuring
that these expectations are clearly outlined and fully supported.

FURTHER READING

Brown, G. (2004). *How Students Learn*. London: RoutledgeFalmer.

Cargill, M. (1996). 'An integrated bridging program for international postgraduate students'. *HE Research and Development*. 15 (2): 177–88.

110

Cryer, P. (1997). 'Handling common dilemmas in supervision: Guide no.2. Issues in postgraduate supervision, teaching and management'. London: Society for Research into Higher Education and the *Times Higher Education Supplement*.

Entwistle, N. J. and Ramsden, P. (1983). *Understanding Student Learning*. London: Croom Helm.

Gibbs, G. (1981). *Teaching Students to Learn*. Buckingham: Open University Press.

Honey, P. and Mumford, A. (1986). *Using Your Manual of Learning Styles*. Maidenhead, Berkshire: Peter Honey Publications.

Kolb, D. A. (1984). *Experiential Learning: Experience as the source of learning and development*. Englewood Cliffs, NJ: Prentice-Hall.

McNamara, D. (ed.) (1997). *Overseas Students in Higher Education*. London: Routledge.

Schmeck, R. R. (1988). *Learning Strategies and Learning Styles*. New York: Plenum Press.

Slaney, K. (1999). 'Models of supervision for enhancing the English language communication skills of postgraduate students'. In G. Wisker and N. Sutcliffe (eds) *Good Practice in Postgraduate Supervision*. SEDA Paper 106. Birmingham: SEDA.

Todd, S. (1997). 'Supervising overseas students: problem or opportunity'. In D. McNamara and R. Harris (eds) *Quality in Higher Education for Overseas Students*. London: Routledge.

Wisker, G. (2000). *Good Practice Working with International Students*. SEDA Paper 110. Birmingham: SEDA.

Zuber-Skerritt, O. (2002). *Supervising Postgraduate Students From Non-English Speaking Backgrounds*. Buckingham: Open University Press.

Chapter 7

Dealing with diversity 2

Academic advice, disability and mental health

With Charlotte Morris

This is the second chapter focused on individual learning support and diversity, the other chapter being Chapter 6. This chapter looks at the academic skills advice and support that you might be called on to provide, and at students with a variety of disabilities and with mental health issues in particular.

ACADEMIC SKILLS SUPPORT

Academic skills support is a specific role in some universities where academic skills advisers are appointed, someone in faculties or schools, sometimes centrally, sometimes both. It is also a role many of us undertake formally or informally as tutors or teachers more generally.

Academic skills and academic advice are often very well supported by one-to-one work, through online study support practices and activities, and through books such as those by Stella Cottrel and others. Considering the focus on the provision of academic skills, Dominic Mahon of Brunel University canvassed members of the growing learning development in HE network (LDHEN) on their work in this area and known provision in universities in the UK. Finding a lack of consensus over the name of the topic and the role, it was decided the definition of 'academic skills will be intended to cover those areas sometimes referred to as study skills or communication skills which include topics such as essay writing, research, numeracy, time management, oral presentations and so on' (Mahon, 2007: 1) and those supporting it would be defined as 'advisers'.

Peelo notes, 'study support staff, then, do not necessarily share a common body of knowledge or agreed methods of working' (Peelo and

Wareham, 2002: 162) and while study support exists in large groups also, one-to-one provision is still a favoured method although there is little consensus over what constitutes good practice. The Oxbridge model is a familiar one. In an interview-based study of the 'Oxford Tutorial', Ashwin (2005) discovered four different conceptions of this form of tuition deriving from 'ideas of the student's role, the nature of the preparation involved, the nature of the material covered, the purpose of the tutorial and even the role of the tutor' (Mahon, 2007: 1).

ESTABLISHING WAYS OF WORKING WITH THE STUDENT

Academic advising or study support is a mixture of facilitation, eliciting and guidance and so employs many of the skills of counselling as a teacher (not as a professional counsellor). Considering the format of individual session where a study support adviser or tutor is working with a student, Cottrell and Main (Cottrell, 2001; Main, 1980) agree sessions should be student centred with the student establishing the areas they wish to work on; any solutions to problems should be elicited from the student rather than diagnosed by the adviser and that some structure is necessary including expectation setting, needs analysis, introduction, rapport forming (Cottrell 2001; Main 1980; Peelo and Wareham, 2002) involving listening, although there is no information or agreement on length and kind of listening.

COUNSELLING AND REFERRAL

Mahon and Cottrell both raise the issue of counselling as an aspect of one-to-one provision although many tutors are wary of describing what they do in this way. Nevertheless, since so much of what is first identified as a study skills or other academic issue often is affected by context, personal, financial and other issues, Cottrell (2001) recommends that advisers take a course in basic counselling techniques. As Peelo and Wareham note:

> What are often called study skills can appear to provide an unemotional, clear-cut means of responding either to those in academic crisis or to those with recognised and specific needs. However the reality of the work is more complex, reflecting struggling students' myriad relationships – academic and non-academic – with their pasts and futures, as well as within the current academic environment
>
> (Peelo and Wareham, 2002: 163)

113

It is vital, however, that tutors know when to refer students to expert sources of help which may include professional counselling within the institution (see Chapter 3 on referring students on). As Student Services is differently organised in different institutions, referral might be quite complex and it is important that advisers have full knowledge of the particular configuration of the university. Mahon's findings, like those of Cottrell, suggest that to consider academic skills tuition as an area of remedial provision in a deficit model of education is misleading. Cottrell notes that students receiving individual academic skills tuition, 'tend to require more intensive support for some or all of their course of study . . . more time and intensive support than could be reasonably expected of lecturers through on-course support' (Paisley and Mahon, 2001: 160). While Mahon notes that at Brunel there is a mixture of students seeking support to pass their course and those that want to improve grades, some seeking merits and distinctions, Peelo also indicates that academic skills provision 'has moved beyond the remedial or deficit model' (Peelo and Wareham, 2002: 161).

TIME AND ISSUES

Academic advising is time consuming and some students return for frequent visits. It is certainly the case that such individual support helps focus them on organising their time, identifying and organising writing tasks and maintaining an overall focus on their work. It is probably not a good idea to develop such a sole relationship that the student becomes dependent on you to help them with the fine detail of white writing and on a very regular basis – referral to others specialised in this help would mean that they start to develop more autonomy once they are more comfortable with their achievements and abilities to focus and get on with their work. There are many good books and websites that will also help students to engage with academic skills, and some elements of self-help under on-site guidance also help foster independence and ownership of the skills/practices.

Mahon's email survey contacted many people who are not themselves study skills providers but educational developers and student services providers, so left the definitions of the academic advice to their appropriate colleagues but it gave an idea of the amount of time spent on academic advising with students – 'the majority of respondents spend at least 2.5 hours a day seeing students on a one-to-one basis. Given an average seven hour working day and allowing for administrative tasks and time between students, it seems fair to say that in the main one-to-one tuition constitutes the majority of academic skills provision. 86% stated that the most common issue that students required assistance with was essay writing and plagiarism. Most respondents (81%) used a combination of students work and their own materials in one-to-one sessions' (Mahon, 2007: 2).

WORKING WITH STUDENTS WHO PRESENT WITH DISABILITIES

One of the benefits of widening participation and the broadening out of the range of students who can access HE is that some students with disabilities or specific learning needs now can develop their potential through studying at university or college. Supporting students with a variety of disabilities might present no issue to you but, on the other hand, you might also feel that you are lacking specialist knowledge or worry about offending the student if you ask questions, and are equally concerned that they might not be getting the help that would then free and enable them to concentrate on their work like any other student.

Students are asked to indicate disabilities on their application forms but not all choose to do so feeling that this might actually operate against rather than for them. So it could be that they present with various disabilities such as visual, motor skills, hearing, mobility and flexibility, affected by illness and physical limitations and you might have had no prior information about this. In some universities tutors working with students with disabilities have a full information sheet sent to explain the kinds of issue that might emerge, arising from that disability, such as difficulties with organisation, time management and so on, and some suggest some ways of addressing these difficulties and needs.

New legislation (Special Educational Needs and Disability Act (SENDA) 2001) now protects equality of educational opportunity, but has somewhat shifted the balance between confidentiality and disclosure. You should, therefore, familiarise yourself with the new Disability Declaration form and associated procedures:

- SENDA 2001 states that if a student discloses a disability to any member of staff, then the institution as a whole is considered to be aware of this and could, therefore, be in breach of its duties if reasonable adjustments are not made in response. However, it is not practical to expect all part-time visiting tutors and non-academic staff to pass on such information to the correct

115

department, and in any case doing so could equally breach the Data Protection Act.

■ Most universities have now introduced procedures to streamline the process of recording and sharing information in an appropriate way. Your role as a personal tutor is to be aware of these procedures and to use them if a student declares a disability for the first time during a tutorial. You should also usually receive a copy of advice from the Disability Team regarding adjustments to teaching or assessment for any students on your list. If you haven't already done so, check that current arrangements are meeting the student's needs.

 ACTIVITY

■ Ensure you are familiar with the systems for supporting students with disabilities at your institution. The central department responsible for this area might have issued guidance for academic staff on procedures, and also on some common adjustments that may be required. If not, you can find some general information and advice for personal tutors from the university or college URL possibly in relation to Student Services.

■ Check that you are aware of any individual students with declared disabilities, so that your initial communications can take this into account. For instance, could a student with a visual impairment cope with the signing-up sheet on your door? If you have a d/Deaf student, will they be lip-reading or working with an interpreter?

■ Consider how to ensure that any students who subsequently develop a disability, such as a long-term illness or mental health difficulties, would feel comfortable about letting you know about this.

■ Make a note of any particular questions you may have about working with disabled students, and discuss these with your departmental liaison tutor and other colleagues.

■ If you need specific advice, talk to the specialist disability staff at your institution.

ASK THE STUDENT

Students who have disabilities are often well aware of exactly what kind of treatment and support will help them get on with their studies. It is important neither to be patronising nor to avoid the disability but better to discuss with them individually and sensitively what kind of person would support them in their learning, whether they would like others in a student group to know about this support need, and what has worked for them in the past. Some universities have networks of disability liaison staff in schools and departments, people who specialise in ensuring that students with disabilities have access to the support and facilities that will enable them to engage fully in their studies. It is worth finding out who such people might be so that you have the information, advice and onwards referral opportunities if possible.

STUDENTS WITH MENTAL HEALTH ISSUES

There has been increased interest in, and research around, student mental health following SENDA 2001, requiring educational institutions to make adjustments for, and in anticipation of, the needs of disabled students, including those with mental health issues.

Given that one in four of the British population suffers from mental health issues in any one year (Mental Health Foundation, 2006), that 18–25 is the age range during which issues are most likely to surface (ibid.) and university life contains many complex stress factors and characteristics that may exacerbate these problems (Royal College of Psychiatrists, 2003) including transition, financial pressures (Roberts and Zelenyanski, 2002) and sometimes high-risk behaviour, it is highly likely that you will come into contact with students with mental health issues during the academic year although these may not always be apparent or disclosed. In the University of Hull Study (Stanley et al., 2000), 35 per cent of academic supervisors reported recent experiences of student mental health problems, 28 per cent of problems described as 'severe' or 'life threatening'.

There is an increasing concern generally about the mental health of young people in particular, a 'Mental Health of Young People' study concluding that the mental health of young people in UK is getting progressively worse (Collishaw et al., 2004). The Samaritans and Centre for Suicide Research (2002) found that one in ten teenagers self-harm at some point and there is concern about increasing rates of young male suicide and barriers to young men, in particular, accessing resources in HE institutions due to stigma attached to using Student Services (Stanley, 2007). A UK Universities/SCOP paper: 'Reducing the risk of student suicide: issues and responses for higher education institutions'(2002) concludes that 'there may be significant risk of suicide and deliberate self-harm amongst a small proportion of the student population in any higher education institution'. However, despite the levels of mental health issues among young people and students, a study carried out at the University of Lancaster (2003) found that 'Many students will not have declared any mental health needs at application or prior to entry. Particularly because of the continuing problems over stigma and mental health in society, this is very commonly the case'.

It is important to be aware that mental health issues can affect anyone and range from mild depression to severe and enduring illnesses or conditions such as clinical depression and bipolar disorder. Sufferers may well experience extended periods of wellness and symptoms might not always be evident. Some students with long-term mental health issues might be experienced in managing their issues and may well feel comfortable discussing their needs openly. If you are worried that a student might be experiencing mental ill-health or that a problem is affecting their well-being or academic progress, do not feel awkward about broaching the subject as they may well appreciate your concern and it could be a first step towards ensuring that the problem does not get out of hand or lead to severe or enduring mental health difficulties. Listening to a problem can be beneficial in itself, as can providing opportunities for students to disclose and for you to refer on to appropriate sources of support (see Chapter 3 on referring students on). It has been suggested that there is a need for a focus on early intervention when problems emerge and that HE institutions should adopt a preventative approach to students developing severe problems (Stanley, 2007). In order for academic staff to adapt their practice in anticipation of the needs of those students experiencing mental health issues, whether long-term or emergent, it is crucial that they develop knowledge and understanding about mental health issues, including the signs and symptoms associated with these including, for example:

- poor health
- poor hygiene
- tiredness
- absence or lateness

- poor concentration
- any uncharacteristic behaviour
- anxiety
- withdrawal
- attention-seeking behaviour.

Mental health issues have a direct effect on the academic progress of many students. The University of Leicester 'Student Psychological Health Project' study (2002) which surveyed over 1,600 students, found that a high proportion (50–60 per cent) of students reported concerns regarding academic progress, particularly in terms of their ability to manage coursework and assessment (60 per cent), the ability to set priorities, make decisions and manage time (59 per cent), concentration (58 per cent) and the ability to meet academic/career goals (63 per cent). Other concerns included adjustment to student life, especially in terms of dealing with inadequate finances (58 per cent), managing psychosocial health (i.e. depression, mood), personal development and relationships. It was estimated that approximately one in six students are likely to be suffering from mental health issues. Grant concludes from the study that widening participation brings a particular set of responsibilities to ensure that 'the learning environment in each institution is as responsive as possible to the needs of the full range of students' (Grant, 2002: 100).

Stigmatisation surrounding mental health, including lack of knowledge and understanding as well as stereotyping and discrimination, has been found to be a major barrier to learning, quality of student experience and accessing support for those experiencing mental health issues. Personal accounts of sufferers' experiences of HE have revealed that stigmatisation surrounding mental health can exacerbate mental health problems and impede academic progress (Brandon and Payne, 2002: 46). A lack of knowledge and understanding of mental health issues was identified by staff at Anglia Ruskin University during the course of the Mind-the-Gap project which sought to improve progression routes into HE. Staff recognised that stigmatisation is the greatest barrier facing students with mental health issues and hoped that this could begin to be addressed through staff development as well as mental health promotion, one member of staff describing the negative stereotyping that can occur:

Inappropriate use of humour and examples of stereotyping of mental health problems in lectures and skills sessions and during fixed resource sessions delivered by some lecturers leave mental health groups of our students (and students across all branches who have personal issues) unable to speak up without a fear of ridicule. Inadvertent humorous and often innocent comments leave the message don't talk about mental health issues here.

(Morris and Lilly, 2006)

Similarly, a researcher concerned with bringing student accounts to bear on mental health issues stated that 'the lack of "visibility" of mental health is one of the most significant barriers to raising awareness and understanding among students and young people' (Wade in Stanley and Manthorpe, 2002: 51). The Royal College of Psychiatrists report *The Mental Health of Students in Higher Education* (2003) states that it is the responsibility of universities to address stigmatisation as under the anticipatory legislation, 'universities must anticipate possible needs and provide a variety of opportunities for confidential disclosure'. Those working one-to-one with students clearly have a vital role in providing these opportunities and engaging in positive, inclusive practice towards those students with mental health issues.

WORKING ONE-TO-ONE WITH STUDENTS WITH MENTAL HEALTH NEEDS

Time spent on one-to-one work with students with mental health issues can be extremely valuable and empowering, potentially enhancing quality in students' learning. As 'mental health issues' incorporates a wide variety of illnesses, conditions, emotional, cognitive and anxiety disorder, and covers the full spectrum of learners with differing learning styles, abilities and support needs, it is difficult to make generalisations. It is important, however, to be aware that mental health issues can affect students' ability to focus, concentrate, organise their work and motivate themselves and that social skills might be affected. Students with perfectionist tendencies may also present cause for concern and need clear, manageable criteria, learning outcomes and expectations, reassurance and praise for their achievements, being particularly vulnerable to mental health issues developing (Stanley, 2007). Tutors and supervisors have an important role to play in identifying students who might be at risk.

For those who find large assignments or projects daunting and overwhelming, it is important in the first instance to break tasks down into manageable chunks and establish a realistic timeframe in which to complete the work with clear, achievable deadlines. Not understanding academic work can be a major source of stress for any student, and providing very clear criteria and realistic expectations is essential here, as is ensuring students have a sound grasp of the study skills required for their subject area. Sensitivity to individual learning styles and providing good, clear supporting materials will further enhance students' confidence and help to reduce stress. Feedback should be positive and constructive, recognising success and providing clear guidelines for development, and it is important for students to have regular opportunities to discuss their progress if they wish to.

As students with certain mental health issues such as anxiety disorders may find it difficult to study in large groups or crowded environments, time spent one-to-one can be vital, as can providing alternative assessment methods where necessary. Furthermore, students with mental health issues are often coping with the side effects of medication, which may cause drowsiness or confusion, affect social skills and make certain times of day difficult; students might be able to concentrate for short periods of time only and might need frequent breaks to drink and/or rest in any learning situation.

It is important to be available, supportive and sympathetic to students with mental health issues and having a helpful and sympathetic tutor with whom to build a trusting relationship can potentially make a positive difference. In the University of Leicester's 'Student Psychological Health Project' study (2002) it was shown that following family and friends (65 per cent), tutors were seen as the most valuable source of support (54 per cent) as opposed to the counselling service (7 per cent). Those working one-to-one with students with mental health issues might, therefore, find themselves with additional pastoral responsibilities in terms of building a positive relationship and ensuring that students are accessing the support they need, including referral when appropriate.

However, while one positive strategy might be to be as available as possible, it is also important to maintain clear boundaries and make it clear when and where you can be contacted and to what extent you are able to assist (see Chapter 3 on referring students on). There is also the issue (discussed earlier in this chapter) of ensuring that students do not become overly dependent on one tutor in terms of their academic work as it is important that they receive specialised help where needed and develop autonomy and confidence – this might be particularly relevant to students with low self-esteem. It needs to be established that the student knows how to access whatever help they need, whether on a personal, social, psychological or academic level and it should be recognised that they might need encouragement and support in accessing Student Services. As previously discussed, while developing basic counselling skills can be beneficial to your teaching practice, it is vital that you know when to refer on to personnel with the appropriate expertise. You should also be aware of personnel who can be contacted for advice and support for yourself should you need it. While the majority of those experiencing mental health issues do not pose a threat to themselves or others, it is vital that you seek help immediately from staff with the appropriate expertise, security staff or emergency services should you feel a student is at risk. For guidance on dealing with difficult behaviour (see Chapter 3 on specialist advice and referrals).

There are many excellent sources of online support, providing invaluable information and resources on a range of mental health issues (some are listed in the further reading section). By building up awareness and knowledge of mental health issues, which any of your students might experience, you can play a valuable role in challenging ignorance and helping to shape positive attitudes towards mental health issues within your own institution and hopefully feel more prepared to respond positively and appropriately when students present with difficulties.

POSITIVE STRATEGIES AND SKILLS FOR WORKING ONE-TO-ONE WITH STUDENTS WITH MENTAL HEALTH ISSUES

Useful strategies and skills include:

- clear instructions and learning outcomes;
- positive communication – acknowledging and valuing contributions;
- listening skills;
- empathy;
- support materials where appropriate;
- sensitivity to learning styles;
- checking understanding;
- awareness of the need for clear time management and management of task;
- ensuring student has access to course information;
- ability to adapt environment where necessary – to make student feel comfortable and secure;
- positive, constructive feedback;

- flexibility in terms of time, structure of the session and assessment;
- regular meetings at a time that is comfortable for the student;
- adopting a consultative rather than authoritarian approach;
- availability, e.g. providing contact details such as email;
- establishing clear boundaries;
- confidentiality;
- referral – study skills, pastoral staff, student advisers, student support services staff such as counsellors, medical/mental health services;
- ensuring the student is aware of the support available to them and encouraging them to utilise it where appropriate;
- ensuring the student is aware of procedures such as mitigation;
- strategies for dealing with students in distress and/or with challenging behaviour;
- knowledge of who to contact for support/in the case of an emergency.

This chapter has considered a range of issues in advising students, the role of the adviser, and in working with the support of students with metal health issues and some physical disabilities. It is a partner chapter to Chapter 6, which considers diversity in terms of learning styles and approaches. Many of the strategies explored in working with diverse learners will be just as useful in working with students in an advice capacity or those with mental health issues and disabilities.

 ## FURTHER READING

Brandon, D. and Payne, J. (2002). 'Breakdown'. In N. Stanley and J. Manthorpe (eds) *Students' Mental Health Needs*. London: Jessica Kingsley.

Cottrell, S. (2001). *Teaching Study Skills and Supporting Learning*. Hampshire: Palgrave.

——— (2003). *The Study Skills Handbook*. Basingstoke: Palgrave Macmillan.

Committee of Vice-Chancellors and Principals of the Universities of the United Kingdom. (2000). *Guidelines on Student Mental Health Policies and Procedures for Higher Education Universities*. London: Committee of Vice-Chancellors and Principals of the Universities of the United Kingdom.

Dewey, J. (1963). *Experience and Education*. New York: Collier.

Doyle, C. and Robson, K. (2002). *Accessible Curricula: Good practice for all*. UWIC Press: Cardiff.

Evans, P. and Varma, V. P. (1990). *Special Education*. London: Falmer.

Grant, A. (2002). 'Identifying students' concerns: taking a whole institutional approach'. In N. Stanley and J. Manthorpe (eds) *Students' Mental Health Needs* (pp. 83–105). London: Jessica Kingsley.

Longley, R. and Wald, M. (undated). *Supporting Students with Mental Health Difficulties*. Southern Higher Education Consortium (SHEC) discussion paper 7. Available from: www.soton.ac.uk/~shec/mentalhealth.htm. Accessed 1 May 2006.

Mahon, D. (2007). 'An investigation into the current nature of one-to-one provision of academic skills in UK higher education institutions'. Brunel University, unpublished.

Morris, C. and Lilly, J. (2006). 'Mind-the-gap report: learning, teaching and access to the curriculum', unpublished.

Peelo, M. and Wareham, T. (2002). *Failing Students in Higher Education*. Buckingham: Open University Press.

Stanley, N. and Manthorpe, J. (eds) (2002). *Students' Mental Health Needs*. London: Jessica Kingsley.

Waterfield, J. and West, B. (2002). *SENDA Compliance in Higher Education; South West Academic Network for Disability Support*. Plymouth: The University of Plymouth.

Youle, C., Hewitt, P., Muston, R. and Read, J. (2000). *Supporting Students with Mental Health Difficulties*. Milton Keynes: Open University.

USEFUL WEBSITES

Depression Alliance: www.depressionalliance.org/. Accessed 2 November 2007.

Government website: www.direct.gov.uk/en/DisabledPeople/HealthAnd Support/MentalHealth/index.htm. Accessed 2 November 2007.

Mental Health Foundation: www.mentalhealth.org.uk/. Accessed 2 November 2007.

Mind: www.mind.org.uk/. Accessed 2 November 2007.

Open University, 'Making your teaching inclusive', section on mental health difficulties: www.open.ac.uk/inclusiveteaching/pages/inclusive-teaching/ recognising-barriers-mental-health-difficulties.php. Accessed 2 November 2007.

Papyrus (Prevention of Young Suicide): www.papyrus-uk.org/. Accessed 2 November 2007.

Samaritans: www.samaritans.org/. Accessed 2 November 2007.

Skill: National Bureau for Students with Disabilities: www.skill.org.uk. Accessed 2 November 2007.

Students in Mind: www.studentsinmind.org.uk/. Accessed 2 November 2007.

Student Mental Health Planning Guidance and Training Manual. S. Ferguson: www.studentmentalhealth.org.uk. Accessed 2 November 2007.

Chapter 8

Supervising and supporting students one-to-one at a distance

Many students are now studying, for part or all of their time with us, at a distance. Their reasons for doing do vary from issues of access, to balancing work and study, to their location. Courses internationally are now constructed, especially at Masters and other postgraduate levels, or for students on franchised courses or at partner colleges, with online tutoring and support built in. The use of online tutoring or support will vary in kind and amount depending on:

- the discipline;
- student needs;
- appropriateness for the learning outcomes;
- availability of appropriate technology skills base of staff and students;
- working with students online and at a distance, whether in a VLE (virtual learning environment) or by audio, video and email contact, involves different kinds of:
  - organisation;
  - timing;
  - pacing;
  - chunking or selecting elements of the work to be engaged with and assessed;
  - interactions – to replace the face-to-face contact.

We need replication of appropriate support and response communications so that the students are not just faced with the course content in paper or e-version and expected to get on with it. Instead, there are online or other electronic communications to support them through their studies.

This book does not attempt to provide a full introduction to online work, but it does look at ways in which we might involve our students working one-to-one, at a distance or using group systems to support the one-to-one work.

Our students are probably going to be far in advance of us in their use of any kind of online discussion and interaction because of their experience of contacting friends on MSN messaging and other sites, and it is useful to build on this experience, involving those less used to online communication by gradually explaining and trialling it with them and asking for peer help in this. Then we need to ensure that there are slightly more formal, boundaried ways of behaving in the online work context, so that social learning takes place, personal space is respected and work gets done.

ONLINE TUTORING

Online tutoring is used by many universities and distance learning organisations and by the Open University in the UK. It can reach students who normally might be unable to access learning because of other commitments, remote living or disabilities, but it does expect certain learning behaviours, protocols, ground rules, boundaries and social interactions in order that it might be successful. (The Online Tutoring Skills OTIS project website, http://otis.scotcit.ac.uk/, still has useful advice.)

Participants in an e-tutoring workshop noted the following distinguishing features of the online learning environment:

- the different nature of interaction between student and tutor;
- the use of a different kind of text – at present, online communication is primarily text- and image-based, and text is presented as spoken text in written 'form';
- the absence of cultural markers (physical appearance, speech and voice, ethnicity, race);
- the need to encourage reflection and deep learning – it is questioned whether the use of technology facilitates 'surface learning'.

In much online learning, contact with the tutor or supervisor will often be augmented by email, Skype, video and phone in different instances.

With the advent of email, videoconferencing, Skype and webcams, it is possible for tutor/mentor/coach and student, or supervisor and research student, and for research or other students in a group, to be in contact over long distances, either on specifically arranged sessions by video-conference, or together through a chat room or a discussion list. Web CT, Blackboard and Moodle online course management systems, among others, provide opportunities for this, for example, as do chat rooms which staff can set up for specific courses, chat groups which students can set up themselves, and Yahoo or other instant messaging systems where you can speak with your student or encourage them to seek support by speaking with others in their tutorial group or working group or other, synchron-ically, i.e. in real time. Alternatively they can talk with you or each other at any time, asynchronically by email. These relatively hi-tech contacts can be used by students wishing to maintain that necessary support from peers, as well as supervisors, or tutors, and to further their studies.

SOCIAL NETWORKING

Social networking is an important aspect of learning for students today. In terms of social networking space it is possible to be in touch with students or encourage them to seek support from each other using social software, which is built on the model of Facebook or Myspace. Social net-working interactions offer the opportunity to make friendly, supportive overtures to students, send basic information, reminders, links, provide a contact for questions about the whole student experience, and give them a space in which to contact you that feels less intrusive and more familiar, perhaps, than via the formal university email. However, Facebook and Myspace, in themselves, are really the students' home spaces and it feels even more intrusive to enter there unless you have, between you, developed an agreement or a community chat group.

At the University of Brighton social networking for the whole student experience and for learning has been built up in an online location called community@brighton, based on the form of Facebook and other social networking. Here, students contact each other about a range of issues including collecting together in groups to relieve the loneliness of being an international student, to watch rugby, to campaign for Green issues and to let each other know what is happening socially and on their courses. This is a staff and student space and staff post up information, quizzes to help induction, and link to course information spaces residing on the university's Blackboard suite named studentcentral. These links are alongside the students themselves talking about events, problems and groups, and so are naturally accessed by the students.

Such use of social networking can extend to pod casts and other contacts to students' mobiles via texting. Much of this is useful to stay in touch and involve groups of students as individuals, and it can be a way for a student with particular questions and needs to find out answers from you or from their peers without having to make a formal appointment or to make the kind of physical face-to-face contact that some students might be shy of. In such instances this new technology can actually help provide support, contact, community and quick interactions one-to-one, online or through mobile technology (the mobile phone).

You might use any of the following to contact your student or for them to contact you and either discuss issues or exchange information or just keep in touch – which is supportive and informative and could well both sort out small immediate issues as well as help maintain an ongoing relationship of trust and interaction without excess intrusion. You might use:

- email;
- Skype;
- webcam;
- videoconferencing;
- Facebook or similar (preferably not their own space but a university/college generated space which is in the same format);
- mobile technology, e.g. pod casts and messages to mobile phones.

USING ELECTRONIC AND VIDEO LINKS TO SUPPORT RESEARCH STUDENTS IN THEIR WORK

Research supervision aided by email and videoconferencing can bring together your distance students joining lone individuals into groups involved in a multimedia videoconference or a Skype conference chat, with or without webcam.

Videoconferencing links and Skype provide the opportunity for students in different locations to offer each other peer support and to share their work or research in progress. Information and ideas can be exchanged with you monitoring the discussion or leaving it to operate on its own depending on intention and outcome. Some of the issues students can discuss will concentrate on joint or individual work or research problems and on trying out ideas and developed projects with each other. Peer comments and support can be rich, especially to the more remote or isolated student. Peers across the world can provide invaluable support for each other and reduce isolation so making your one-to-one work with each student a richer experience for each of them. In the context of international students, there can be a fascinating breadth of knowledge and approaches that spring from the different learning cultures of students of different nationalities and locations and they can support each other, exchange ideas and build ongoing communities while you observe and enter discussions if asked, knowing this builds independence too. Students can put each other in touch with reading materials, resources and links in a number of countries, as well as keeping valuable contacts that could be most useful in the years after they have finished their studies or completed their research.

DIFFERENT MODES OF CONTACT

Audio conferencing and Skype conferencing

Students can book audio and Skype conferences with each other to carry on work-in-progress discussions without the presence of the supervisor, or you as supervisor or tutor can conduct a moderated discussion between your students by chairing a conference call.

Email

This is by far the most common and the easiest form of staying in touch with individual students and then joining them in with other individuals on an email discussion list. For individual students, access to the email can provide an invaluable discussion forum.

The formal email discussion group can be set up and joined by students around the campus and off-site, working from home, students with disabilities and those who are less forthcoming in class and, for research students, by researchers around the world. You can set up an informal group to which students are invited or there can be a more formal closed group with students subscribing to be involved in it and closed discussions taking place among the group. Emails are good for asynchronous discussion (though it can also host fast and furious returns and discussions almost synchronously).

Instant messaging

Immediate lively discussion is best facilitated through instant messaging and in discussion groups using synchronous chat activities. MSN and other messaging services can be useful for students to join, with you to facilitate or to stand back and encourage their engagement over set issues and just supply study support.

Such support uses group processes to involve individuals and so minimises the demands on your time, but also enables students to deal with issues and surface problems and questions to deal with or share with you later.

Synchronous discussion and asynchronous discussion are useful in keeping in touch. A useful and more distant involvement can also be maintained, where you read others' comments and only contribute if you have something to say, but remain in touch nonetheless. This version of asynchronous discussion is enabled by being connected through Web CT or Blackboard and students and tutor meet in the chat room space of the course or module site. There, they also have access to course documents and work outlines so can move between discussion with you and each other, and then materials they need for their work if they are either accessing these remotely or revising and re-accessing them.

Really profitable learning conversations can take place in a chat room even though the language is casual and the issues discussed might range between serious work questions and social comments. The 'chat room' can act as a virtual tutorial discussion space. Students can post comments on work in progress and ask for support and tips from others in their tutorial class or research group. You as tutor can facilitate this or join in and help solve some problem or provide tips, but the main discussion and support comes from the students themselves, to each other.

Email feedback

Because email is such a common form of communication now it is probable your individual student will be asking you for support with the development of their work and then feedback on the email either informally or formally. It is best not to give summative formal feedback in this way unless it is through a normal electronic system such as the Open University's etma (electronic tutor marked assignments) system, as it can be open to misinterpretations and abuse if too casual. However, formative comments are useful and providing feedback to students on their work in progress through email can be done in several ways.

Setting some ground rules about email exchanges, when you can answer emails and what kinds of advice, support and feedback are impossible given security, and your time, is important here. You can work with:

- *Short responses* – these can be exchanges, short emails with bullet point lists of ideas and suggestions and comments, in answer to short questions.
- *Longer responses* – involved in commenting on the work itself, either work in progress or the final documents sent, using the functions 'track changes' – to substitute, cut, alter, enhance and rephrase expression and see what further work has been added or altered – and 'comment' – to make notes or suggestions, or provide hints, tips and links to further reading. With the tool 'comments' your comments can be woven in and the student needs to decide what to do to the work, but with 'track changes' your words can be substituted for the student's work, and the temptation is for the student to merely accept your changes. This is sometimes acceptable but only for short rephrasings to help, otherwise it looks as though your work is largely an editing role. It's probably better for the student's actual learning to rephrase according to your suggestions rather than merely accept everything you would put in instead. It is possible to work in detail on a particular paragraph, section or page in 'track changes', changing it minutely, and to then indicate to the student, using 'comments', that they should take the level of this response and changes further on through the rest of the work itself.

Feedback on written work or drafts

Feedback to encourage writing that is critically informed, well-argued and well-expressed is essential for the development of good essays/project reports/theses/dissertations. But do beware of the tone of online comments and feedback on texts if you are unlikely to be able to talk it through with your student face-to-face, as the tone is often an issue and can be misinterpreted, especially if the student is from another cultural learning group, or is international and/or working at a distance. Some tutors and supervisors can seem over-harsh and critical in their comments especially when delivered online, through an email, using track changes and comments or other distance means. Sometimes these comments can seem terse, a little vague, rather thin, so excessive as to overwhelm the student so that they might be confused as to which aspect of the work to deal with first. Some students report confusion at being given a paragraph that is heavily corrected, with a few guiding points and then being told to go on and take such a level of change through the whole chapter. This is, in fact, hard to handle the first time the student is asked to do it, but if you clarify and model what is expected they should soon become familiar with what is wanted. You could also spend some time explaining tone in email and feedback so that there are fewer confusions and you could invite your student to ask for clarification if they are unsure of what you are saying.

It is a good idea with distance communication to explain what you mean or avoid cryptic or confusing comments, such as:

- Please clarify.
- Not sure what you mean here.

Avoid vague comments that suggest further work or reading but don't indicate how much:

- Say more.

It is probably a good idea to give them an example or model of what you want here — and suggest further reading and what to look for in it rather than just:

- Look at Biggs.

Instead: 'Try Biggs (1991), he has interesting things to say about the "myth of the Asian learner" when he notes that the argument about memorisation of work fails to take into account that there are different forms of memorisation of which some definitely aid deep learning. He says on p. 6, ". . .".'

Avoid the veiled threats of failure:

- Conceptually weak.
- No!

And instead consider ways of exploring what you mean so you could instead say: 'Can you develop the conceptual level here, i.e. what ideas and theories are underpinning your argument? How does what you are saying engage with ideas and theories here?'

133

If you want to generally suggest a satisfied response do also indicate what it is that you are celebrating:

- Lots of interesting work here.
- Yes!

These are rather vague 'phatic' comments and need to be followed by specific comments about the area you are looking at and specific advice, including examples of good expression. Comments that model ways of re-writing, that prompt thinking and suggest examples of alternatives can aid the student's thinking especially in an online or distance environment where you have to simulate your discussion together. These include phrases such as:

- Someone else might argue that . . .
- It could be said that . . .
- In what ways could this be said to be . . .?
- If this is the case, what follows and what might this mean?

Frameworks for writing are useful for students as they proceed at a distance so using prompts to help identify and suggest ways of dealing with problems, critique, critical evaluation and conceptualisation in thinking and writing can all help them to develop and minimise the need for your intrusion later on.

Rowena Murray makes some useful suggestions about feedback:

> You may have been expecting more feedback on what you think of as the 'content', but they see the use of terms – and assessing whether or not you can use them properly – as a priority. You can regard this as a tension between what you expect and what you get. Or you can accept that you have work to do – and who would not have – in clarifying what you have written.
>
> (Murray, 2002: 78)

Selective feedback and hierarchies of feedback can enable students to focus on some issues at a time. *Models* of writing required are very useful if the student needs to write at a different level and in a different way. You can offer them examples of the successful work of others or work that is published but in a similar format to the work required of them in an essay, such as journal essays. Ask students to read through and 'process' the writing, i.e. consider how it is written in terms of the level of expression (rather than focusing on the sense – rather, see how it is said), and then see how this can inform their own writing development.

TONE AND COMMUNICATIONS

Whether sending emails, chatting in an online chat room or assessing work using comments and track changes, it is all too easy to accidentally send an online or email exchange or comment that is misunderstood, especially if you do not have a well-established method of communicating with each other from face-to-face interactions and if there is cultural difference as well as distance involved. You need to develop some agreed guidelines of interaction and behaviour through the email exchanges. Is it a quick question to deal with in between classes or at any time of the day or a longer question, the checking of a piece of work in progress, draft chapters to be considered, a questionnaire to be looked through and commented on and so on? Students need to know these take different lengths of time and that you are not always available.

We need to learn to manage our time and interactions and our expectations. As a tutor it is overwhelming to be sent vast quantities of material requiring detailed attention followed up by a request for immediate response, or work sent at awkward times.

 ACTIVITY

Consider:

- Do you have, or could you have, access to videoconferencing or audio-conferencing for distance tutorials and supervisions?
- Do you have, or could you have, access to these conferencing methods for discussion with other research students?
- Do you or could you use email to discuss your work with your supervisor? How?
- Do you or could you become involved in an email discussion group, or join a mail-base discussion group or Web CT (or other) chat room?
- Do you have access to instant messaging, or Skype?
- If so, which ones are likely to be helpful and appropriate for you?
- How might you best use these different forms of contact?

135

Ask students to indicate the required response to the kind of email they are sending, e.g. 'quick question' or 'longer response', with some indication of what is being sent — questionnaire to look over, draft chapters, abstract and so on — and reply giving them an idea of when you can respond. It is up to us as tutors to agree such rules and protocols with them.

Set up ground rules about turnaround times. Set up virtual office hours and keep to them so students are aware of when they can contact you and how long it will take for a response, and you can ensure you have time to produce a considered response.

USEFUL WEBSITE

Online Tutoring Skills (OTiS) Project Website: http://otis.scotcit.ac.uk/. Accessed 2 November 2007.

Chapter 9

Helping students help themselves

Peer support

As tutor, coach, mentor or supervisor you are not the only person who is able to work with, and enable, students to get on successfully with their work and in the full student experience. There are many services in the university or college that will support you in this and to which students can turn for different needs. One of the great benefits of working in an institution is the support services, however they are constituted. These systems and individuals are vital for the students' experience.

You are also not alone in your working with students because of the existence of both formal and informal peer support systems.

SUPPORTING STUDENTS TO HELP THEMSELVES

One of the most useful things you can do to help students for whom you have a one-to-one responsibility is to help build their capacity to help themselves. There are several approaches to this (not mutually exclusive):

■ encouraging peer support and sharing of work processes in formal practices through group work, work-in-progress seminars or similar, or as a part of courses;
■ encouraging peer support through student-led elements of tutorial support, action learning sets that run themselves;
■ working with students in a teaching and learning support model such as through SI, peer assisted learning (PAL) and mentoring;
■ encouraging peer support in informal or less formal practices such as buddying systems;

- building on processes now normally associated with PDP encouraging them to be more autonomous and systematic in their approach to their own personal development.

MORE FORMAL PEER SUPPORT

Peer support can be organised as part of studying, in the shape of a study group or group learning, mentoring (see Chapter 4) or supplemental instruction, and peer assisted learning (see Chapter 4), all of which involve students in supporting each others' learning and sharing learning tasks. All of the systems rely upon the theory and practice of sharing, working together in peer groups, critical friendship, and, in some instances, the broader and deeper theories of communities of practice (Lave and Wenger, 1999). They are also informed by what we know from the literature about retention, student engagement with the local learning processes of a university or college through the bonds and social networks that they can make, social learning more generally and the many systems of buddying, peer support, groupwork, supplemental instruction and mentoring. All of these systems and practices form part of the map of the social learning and peer support that augment and enhance your own one-to-one work with your students. There is a wealth of literature (Yorke, 1998) that indicates that social and peer learning not only helps support students in their work and so augments the support you are providing, but helps to build networks, communities and a well-rounded, exciting, pleasant, stimulating and nurturing student experience.

 ACTIVITY

Consider:

- Who would the natural supportive peer group be for your students on your course?
- How can you help set up a support group?
- Is there one you could suggest that your students join?
- Are there peers with whom your students could work and exchange ideas, and work in progress? This is particularly useful for those who are engaging in research and need to share ideas and critique each others' work.

SUPPLEMENTAL INSTRUCTION (SI)

This more formal form of support by peers was developed in many contexts, the University of Kingston and Oxford Brookes among others. The theory behind it is of students further on in their learning careers working with those who are a year below them, to part teach, support, encourage and enable the students to engage successfully with their work (see Chapter 4).

SELF-MANAGED GROUPS AND NETWORKS AS PART OF THE FORMAL LEARNING

Some courses involve group learning and some also use group assessment. Groups who are naturally working together on similar projects or tasks, and, with research students, those who are working with the same supervisor or close colleagues as supervisors, or in a project group completing a piece of (usually) scientific or Social Science research together, can all benefit from the supportive group activities and the level of critique that such a group can afford. All students can benefit. In the case of research students, more commonly in the Arts and Humanities where research projects are a lone venture, if there is no natural grouping of research students around a project, then it is important that supervisors, you and other students, work to draw others together.

Meeting together in self-help, peer-group sessions can provide support, the opportunity to share ideas and work in progress and receive critiques and suggestions from peers involved at the same level, perhaps the same stage in their work, and who can themselves learn from and hear about each others' questions, methods, problems and achievements. If you are helping to set up or maintain such a group, you will need to ensure there is an extra social element, because this enhances the student learning experience, makes it less stressful and contributes to their likelihood of staying on the course, finishing the project and being active learners, able to communicate with and share with others; all good graduate skills.

TUTORIAL SUPPORT GROUPS (TSGs)

Fellow students will often be an even more valuable source of help and advice in a student's time at university. This will happen informally as they make friends and get to know the other students on their course and elsewhere.

In addition to this natural process, some courses, such as Visual Culture at the University of Brighton, encourage the setting up of slightly more formal student-managed tutorial groups, which meet at regular intervals to provide mutual support. They have many potential benefits and an expanded discussion of these benefits, ways of setting up and maintaining tutorial support groups, and guidelines for running them successfully follows.

On Visual Culture, all the students who share the same personal tutor in each year automatically constitute a TSG. These groups are encouraged to meet regularly at a mutually convenient time, inside or outside college premises, to discuss the course, share problems and solutions and generally help each other to get the most out of the programme. Because these groups are intended to be run by and for the students themselves, the course team tries not to interfere too much in their organisation. However, to help them get started and get used to meeting regularly, some Part One projects may be based on tutorial groups. In addition to lectures and seminars, staff have timetabled group meetings for project work and occasional talks and course reviews. After Part One, students decide how they want to organise their group so it still meets on a regular basis.

What are the aims of tutorial support groups?

TSGs aim to provide a supportive environment in which students can:

- view the course as a whole;
- review their own and others' progress;
- share ideas and experience on research, working methods, time management;
- develop communication skills;
- develop critical abilities;
- anticipate and prepare for tutorials, assessments and examinations.

This might involve:

- identifying the areas where they need help – to use staff time more effectively;
- practising seminar presentations within a small group;
- sharing and discussing background reading;

140

- brainstorming ideas for essays;
- revising together for exams;
- bringing common problems or queries to the attention of the course team.

Students who have participated in self-managed groups have identified the following benefits:

- developing skills in listening and giving and receiving feedback;
- practising critical evaluation of their own and others' work in a safe environment;
- learning to manage meetings effectively;
- generating creative ideas and solutions to problems;
- setting and achieving personal goals;
- taking responsibility for their own learning;
- building self-confidence.

How can students run the group successfully?

During the first two terms, any meetings mainly relate to induction work and project preparation. After that, however, it is important to structure meetings so that time is not wasted, otherwise people won't be committed to attending on a regular basis. A simple framework can help, allowing everyone an equal opportunity to focus on the issues that are important to them and avoiding meetings being dominated by the most talkative students. At the start students may want to agree some ground rules – for instance:

- that it is each person's responsibility to attend meetings;
- that each person is to have an equal amount of time to talk without interruption;
- they will talk about their work or their current concerns (they might appoint a timekeeper to help with this);
- that at the end of a meeting, each person agrees on something they want to work on, get help with, or achieve, by the next meeting. This can be the starting point for next time;
- that if tutors are invited to attend for a specific purpose, they observe the ground rules; and
- no one should try to lead the meeting.

141

There are two widely used ways to organise these groups. Either students can agree in advance on a particular topic for each session, such as time management, seminar presentations, background reading, essay writing, exam revision, etc. Alternatively, they divide up the available time between them and deal with whatever comes up. This is not practical with very large groups, which may prefer to split into two groups of around five people each. Some groups operate a combination of these two patterns, giving everyone a few minutes at the start to raise any individual concerns, but then using the bulk of the time to discuss whatever common issues seem most important. Each group will eventually evolve a format that works well for them.

So what happens at a typical meeting?

What follows is based on a group who use most of their time for individual contributions and is directed at your students to consider for their own use.

1   *It is usual to start by agreeing the length of the meeting (e.g. ninety minutes).* Consider whether there are any special needs or deadlines? There is no leader, chairperson or formal agenda. If it is the first meeting, agree any ground rules (such as confidentiality). Decide who will go first, second, etc.

2   *Appoint a timekeeper each time.* Their job will be to manage the meeting to ensure that each person has an equal amount of time for discussion about their coursework or whatever issues are important to them.

3   *Divide up the time.* e.g. in a ninety-minute meeting, five minutes at the start to appoint timekeeper, etc., fifteen minutes each for five people, leaving ten minutes to review the tutorial and fix the time and place for the next meeting.

4   *Review progress and get feedback.* During each person's allotted time they have the chance to outline their progress since the last meeting, and refer to the action points agreed last time. They raise issues of concern to them, seek help or feedback from other members, e.g. 'I can't seem to get started with this essay . . .', 'I'm getting behind with my reading . . .', 'I can't decide how to focus my seminar presentation . . .' or even 'I can't get up in the mornings . . .'. During this time, other people can

142

help clarify ideas and offer constructive comments, but should not take over someone else's slot with 'me too' accounts of their own experiences.

5   *Agree at least one action point for each person.* The timekeeper should indicate when each person's time is nearly up so you can spend the last few minutes agreeing at least one *specific* action point, to be achieved by the next meeting. For instance: to seek help from a tutor about a particular problem, to keep a note of time spent on different tasks, or to get up early for a week! Action points must be realistic and achievable for the individual concerned. You may also discover common issues that can be dealt with collectively, such as working on your note-taking technique by comparing lecture notes on a regular basis.

6   *Review how the meeting went.* Each meeting will end with a review of how it went – for example, was it useful; did people feel they had a fair amount of time to discuss issues important to them; did they receive the kind of feedback and help they were looking for; what themes, if any, might they want to identify for the next meeting?

7   *You might want to keep a record.* This is not essential but some people find it helps them to focus if they keep a note of the action points or the issues discussed, and each keep a copy to refer back to at the next meeting.

You may also wish to feed back any general comments or queries to the course team, either via your personal tutor or directly to the course leader. This can be a more immediate way of dealing with issues than waiting for the next course committee.

8   *Preparation.* Obviously meetings will be more productive if participants think about what help/feedback they want from each other and come to meetings prepared with ideas, work in progress, essay plans, etc. Or groups might decide to work on something specific at a meeting, for example, discussing seminar presentations or exam revision.

9   *How can you review your progress without a tutor's help?* It can be helpful to spend some of your first meeting drawing up a simple checklist of aspects of your coursework that you might want to look at (e.g. time management, general organisation, written assignments, seminar presentations, critical diary, etc.). You could also use tutors' comments on your coursework as a starting point. When someone else is discussing a particular issue, try to comment in a way that helps them clarify their position and reach their

own solution rather than just telling them what you think they should do, as everyone needs to work in their own way. However, airing a problem and finding it is shared can result in a pooling of ideas for solutions, some of which may be appropriate for you.

10   *Tutors' roles*. After terms 1 and 2, you should not wait for the course team to arrange your meetings for you, although they may wish you to confirm that you are meeting regularly. Students may wish to invite tutors, usually for a specific purpose (e.g. to clarify some aspect of the course, or to run a workshop on study skills). If staff agree to come, they should be acquainted with the ground rules and should not lead the session. Students are responsible for managing their own meetings.

This model of self-managed student support towards work outputs is one that can be translated into many different contexts with students setting up their own less formal support groups, developing such groups out of a formal setting where they are not normally in existence. The important elements are your initial support and staying in touch, student management, and their working within the agreed boundaries and ground rules.

PEER SUPPORT SYSTEMS FOR RESEARCH STUDENTS

All of the group support systems that are possible for undergraduates are similarly possible for postgraduates, but postgraduates do differ in that they might be more isolated because they are involved in lone projects (Arts and Humanities) or they might be working part time or at a distance, juggling study with work and domestic responsibilities (though this also is true of many undergraduate students now).

Possible group support systems include:

■   setting up support groups close by and at a distance;
■   work-in-progress and seminar presentations;
■   building academic communities of practice for sustainability in different cultural contexts.

Although research students are expected to work largely autonomously, with supervision, they are also entering a large local, national and international 'community of practice' (Lave and Wenger, 1999) when they begin to research. Increased international communications and the internet means we can all be more in touch with each other, supportive, exchanging ideas, contacts and work in progress and this includes the research students. You can:

- put your student in touch with others at a distance – whether other students or experts in the field (check they are happy to be contacted);
- help set up a nurturing distance community of researchers talking to each other and developing work together or just sharing their ideas and achievements (and difficulties). Many questions can be answered, stress relieved, and clarification gained by working together in various supportive peer groups close by or at a distance. Ultimately, by putting students in touch with each other to support each other at a distance or locally, you could be helping to set up research partnerships for the future from such support groups.

Some supportive groups develop because students are working together in a research team. More often, they develop because they decide to set up groups to exchange questions, developments and progress, or supervisors bring groups together in the first instance and then, like TSGs, expect them to run by themselves with occasional contacts with you as supervisor.

Group/project team supervisions

In some subject areas, such as practical Science or Medicine, there are likely to be several students working on a related project. In these cases it would be useful to encourage students to organise regular group project supervisions where they can share ideas, problems and questions, and general problems can be shared and overcome, thus leaving specific needs for discussion one-to-one.

Research in progress seminars

More formally this sharing and critiquing of work, particularly among research students, could develop into a system of research-in-progress seminars. In seminars students each share research questions, developments, work so far, questions, problems and achievements, and seek ideas, critical questions and suggestions about analysis or further reading from each other.

When they present work to the group it needs to be in a managed and comprehensible shape, and this forces research students to organise and clarify thoughts, defend their choices of methodology and methods, order their data and interpret them, and produce results they can share with others, and the arguments they can try out with an audience of their peers. It also takes some of the initial weight of critiquing and making suggestions from you as they can address many issues, and clarify their work before they bring it to you. Presentation to peers is a marvellous opportunity for students to use the critical thinking of others who are working in similar areas, using similar methodologies or even working in totally different areas but involved in the processes of research. All kinds of questions about questionnaire wording, viability of research samples, how to interpret data, and the status, clarity and quality of their own writing can be shared first in such a group, then with you.

Students sharing their work is also part of entering the community of academic colleagues and academic debate and presentation at a work-in-progress seminar is also a practice or 'dry' run for later conference presentations, and even the viva if they are undertaking a UK or European Ph.D. Working together in supportive peer groups, they can also move beyond the Ph.D. or Master's in itself, can circulate information about conferences and publication opportunities, even job vacancies to each other, so expanding a research culture that could extend beyond the project.

Exploratory talk, working at a conceptual level and critiquing work are all important parts of such exchanges between research students.

INTERNATIONAL STUDENTS: UNDERGRADUATES AND POSTGRADUATES

For international students, such a self-help, research support or other work-oriented group might well be set up initially by the international office, the faculty or school office, you as tutor or supervisor or the postgraduate school if there is one. Some international students and others who have moved a considerable distance to undertake their studies, even bringing family with them or leaving them behind, could find study or research life very lonely and a support group is a social as well as an intellectual 'lifeline'.

Although the tutor or supervisor plays a key role in setting up such self-managed groups and networks to begin with, the groups should then be able to run on their own, driven by the students, because they are useful to them. This is essential supportive networking and it is up to the students to work together to establish and continue it.

Communities of practice, local and international, can be established and maintained beyond the life of the research projects, and in many instances academic research can cause real change in certain contexts through some communities, leading to the sustainable development of research, changes in a variety of practices, and so the research, supported by the ongoing community, can have a real impact on culture, society, behaviour and human knowledge.

PEER PAIRING

Tutors and supervisors can set up systems of peer pairing where students, including research students, are put in touch with each other to work together supportively in pairs. They do not have to be working on the same project, but should be involved in similar subject areas or using similar methodologies. They might both be students of the same supervisor or of her/his colleagues. For the new student or research student, being paired formally with another who has more experience or who is also new, can be most helpful. They will, in time, make their own contacts and friends, but the supportive pairing ensures that they meet regularly with another person and compare notes and information ideas, overcoming some problems. This relieves some of the initial burden of work from the tutor or supervisor, who can then concentrate on supervising the project or the student's work, their dissertation, or thesis and its needs rather than spending much of the time repetitively passing on information.

PEER SUPPORT SYSTEMS OVER A DISTANCE

An increasing number of research students, in particular, are working at a distance, carrying out their research at home or in a country different from that of their supervisor. Sometimes although the expertise is in a country other than their own and it would be enriching to study there, family ties, work ties and finances make it difficult to move, so they need to study at a distance and we need to ensure that there is support not only one-to-one but with peers for such work. See Chapter 8 on working at a distance to consider how to support such students, adding in the practice

147

of putting them in touch with each other so that they can discuss their work online, in chat rooms or MSN or via Facebook or the university's social networking such as community@brighton in the case of the University of Brighton.

BUDDY SYSTEMS

These have operated in many universities and colleges and originated in the US. Students who are new to the university, from international contexts, who have particular learning needs, or who would just find it supportive and useful to have someone with some experience of the systems and practices of the university, who is willing to talk with them and pass on information and networks, would find a buddy system very useful. You can set up a buddy system within a course or programme, or it could be organised centrally by Student Services or the Students' Union.

We have looked at a variety of formal and informal support systems for students to help themselves whether they are undergraduates or postgraduates, international students studying at a distance or in your own institutions, students with particular learning needs. All students can benefit from taking some of the responsibility for running paired relationships or groups that help support and develop their work, and the skills they develop in doing this mutual support can transfer usefully to their working lives after university.

PEER ASSISTED LEARNING

Another form of support between students is PAL or SI where students support each others' work or where students further on in their work career support the work of students earlier in their career. There have been many studies of this in different contexts. Those offering the support can be:

- paid/given credit;
- encouraged to use the experience for their PDP portfolios.

There are many benefits in PAL and SI if managed properly as it, like mentoring, can provide the one who assists with a range of skills and it is often preferable for one student to gain their study support from another who has recent insights in the expectations and ways forward.

PAL operates usually by using trained second- or third-year students, working alone or in pairs, to supervise the learning of a small group of first-year students using a classroom-based model or small-group model. In a study of PAL, Capstick (2004) suggests a wide range of benefits for both student participants and PAL leaders from involvement in a PAL scheme but there are potential shortcomings.

PAL can lead to increased retention as students are more confident, support each other and feel more involved with university life, especially during the first year (Wallace, 2004).

 FURTHER READING

Burkitt, I., Husband, C., Mackenzie, J., Torn, A. and Crow, R. (2001). *Nurse Education and Communities of Practice. Researching professional education*. London: ENB.

Gibbs, G., Wisker, G. and Bochner, B. (1999). *Supporting More Students*. Oxford: Oxford Brookes University.

Hildreth, P., Kimble, C. and Wright, P. (2001). 'Computer mediated communications and international communities of practice'. Conference proceedings of the 1998 Ethicomp. Rotterdam: Erasmus University.

Lave, J. and Wenger, E. (1999). 'Legitimate peripheral participation in communities of practice'. In R. McCormack and C. Poechter (eds) *Learning and Knowledge* (pp. 21–35). London: Paul Chapman Publishing.

Wenger, E. (2000). 'Communities of practice and social learning systems'. *Sage*, 7 (2): 225–46.

—— and Lave, J. (1991). *Situated Learning*. Cambridge: Cambridge University Press.

Yorke, M. (1998). 'Assessing capability'. In J. Stephenson and M. Yorke (eds) *Capability and Quality in Higher Education* (pp. 174–91). London: Kogan Page.

Chapter 10

Supervising postgraduates in the Social Sciences, Arts and Humanities

For many of us, the supervision of postgraduates is an expectation and an experience that almost immediately follows the achievement of our own Ph.D., and for others it is something we move gradually towards, depending on experience and opportunity. It could well feel like one of the peaks of your career, as it offers an opportunity to match thoughts and cognitive processes, and work on projects, with students who have a real interest in areas in which you have expertise – whether in the subject or in the methodology and methods (or both). You might already have some experience in supervising at undergraduate level, or in the workplace, and you have certainly had experience in being supervised yourself, so drawing on this experience is a useful piece of groundwork. The postgraduate students you supervise have already, to some extent, proved (at undergraduate level) that they can undertake research successfully through to completion, writing up and presenting it in acceptable form. However, for both you and your students working together for the first time, whether you have supervision experience or not, this is a new venture, since every student is an individual with his or her own learning needs, every Master's or Ph.D. research project is somewhat different, and every supervisory relationship is a human, one-to-one interaction, so there are always issues, strategies, processes and relationships to take into account in the equation of successful supervisory practice. To students there are great learning leaps to be made between the undergraduate dissertation or project and postgraduate Master's work, and again at Ph.D. level, mainly to do with conceptual depth, contribution to knowledge, as well as, of course, in relation to length and scope.

This chapter looks at supervision of postgraduate students in the Arts and Humanities, the Social Sciences and subjects that use Social Science methodologies and methods, such as business and management, and healthcare practice. Chapter 11 looks at supervision in the Sciences. Both also contain generic comments and suggestions.

KEY ISSUES: SUPERVISION AS LEARNING AND TEACHING INTERACTION

We might feel we need to supervise in the same way as we were ourselves supervised. This is fine if we were supervised well – but it is useful to look at some of the research evidence-based work on supervisory processes and practices to consider how we might work with our very different postgraduate learners in order to best enable and empower them to achieve their research outcomes, passing the Master's or the Ph.D. examination and, in the case of the Ph.D., the viva.

Perhaps you and your student might feel that here are two experts working together in a collegial fashion, and the less you intrude on their research, the better. You might find your student expects to get on with the project alone, but you might also find that he or she has very high expectations of your guidance right from the point of choosing a topic and question through to each step of developing research methods and vehicles such as questionnaires, and drawing any kind of interpretation of findings or conclusions from the data. It is a good idea to avoid such potentially great differences in your mutual expectations, experiences and expertise, right from the start, so that guilt, anxiety, confusion, stunted progress and general breakdowns in communication and activity never even begin to arise. To this end, I am going to suggest that we take supervision and research processes as a learning and teaching process, one that is based on mutual respect and leads to shared expertise, and collegiality, as well as a satisfactory outcome in terms of the quality of the completed research and the success of the dissertation or thesis at examination and beyond.

SOCIAL SCIENCES, ARTS AND HUMANITIES – SIMILARITIES AND DIFFERENCES

There are many similarities between Social Sciences, Arts and Humanities research supervision, but to see differences we will look also at postgraduate supervision generally and consider what kinds of differences emerge, then focus very specifically on those differences towards the end of the chapter.

151

SUPERVISING THE SOCIAL SCIENCES

Social Science students work with people and people's behaviours and interactions, sometimes in terms of interaction between large numbers of people and social phenomena, sometimes charting change and response to them, and sometimes observing or charting specific responses and reactions at a point in time, perhaps in response to a problem, a change in circumstance, or a specific set of cultural, social, economic and political circumstances. In this respect, it is people-based, real-world research, although often it might well deal in statistics to identify large-scale responses rather than in individualised personal responses.

Social Science students are engaged in a project that needs to be well structured, carefully timed and absolutely explicit in terms of the methodology and methods used. Much of our supervision of Social Science students is concerned with ensuring that the research question or hypothesis is identified clearly, and that theoretical perspectives and methodology and methods flow logically from the question in order to enable the student to address the question or answer it, and test the hypothesis. Using the word hypothesis might seem strange here as this is not usually an experimental mode as such. Unlike Science students, Social Science students are not usually actually experimenting, although they might well be using a group of people who go through a programme, an experimental type of experience, and whose responses are assessed, somewhat like a scientific piece of research.

ETHICS

Because Social Science students are engaged in research on and with people, the issue of ethics is very important, as it is with health and scientific researchers. Even if you are not causing any potential harm to anyone with this research, or at least not in any planned way, you will still need to seek ethics approval because your work is in some way connected with people. More on ethics, below.

DIFFERENCES BETWEEN SOCIAL SCIENCES AND ARTS AND HUMANITIES

The main differences between the Social Sciences and the Arts, is that the Social Sciences are dealing with people in interactions in a culturally, historically and socially inflected context. Ethics are almost always involved unless your student is undertaking a highly theorised piece of research, e.g. on the difference between Social Science theorists and their views. Other differences include the methodology and methods to enable the research to take place.

SUPERVISING HUMANITIES AND ARTS

Much Arts and Humanities research involves the identification of a research question and its cultural and historical context, but it is unlikely to involve human subjects in the same way that Social Science research does. However, some students undertaking literature-based research might deal with autobiography as a literary form, and in that way, the confidentiality and ethics issues and practices relevant in the Social Sciences are equally relevant here. Arts and Humanities students might also seek responses from human subjects in some other instances, as in personal narrative taking in history, or using views of great writers as one element in the critical discussion of their work.

Those involved in video or art practice could well be basing their work on, and with, human subjects and so might need substantial ethics approval, as would a social scientist. In this instance, the choice of the research question, theoretical perspectives and the choice of appropriate methodology and methods resemble the same kind of task and same kind of choices seen in Social Sciences research, so supervision of these students and the shape of their research would closely resemble that of the social scientist. However, there are some instances where Arts and Humanities students are involved in research that does differ from that of social scientists, and where the actual shape of the thesis or dissertation and the methods used are quite unsuited to a Social Science thesis and the kind of defence and management that supervisors need to ensure their student attends to in the Social Sciences.

Students studying the Arts and Humanities are quite often undertaking research that enables them to be creative; some others are using archives, editing formats, undertaking primary or secondary historical research with artefacts and analysis. Many of these research processes used by the Arts and Humanities resemble those of the Social Sciences: asking research questions, problematising reading of events and practices, asking research questions of what some take for granted and opening up areas of knowledge. Other issues and practices emerge in the use of critical practice in relation to established texts and readings, access to information and critique. Humanities and Arts research might well involve the personal, and subjective, a creative response to a research question or problem. But it will also involve rigour in research processes, analysis and careful matching of what is claimed to what is shown, i.e. claim and evidence, even in the case of, for example, an Arts student using their creative writing as the body of their Ph.D., where their discussion and analysis of the intentions, development, drafting changes and the achievement of the work in terms of form and realisation in the work, are all as rigorous as any defence of an argument based on statistics might be, or the argument based on analysis of interview data.

Students engaged in literary theses are more likely to be undertaking reading than engaging with human subjects. Their primary sources are the work of the author, their secondary sources critical commentaries on these cultural and historical contexts rather than methodology and methods, although where students maintain specific critical positions, such as structuralism, feminism, Marxism, deconstruction, queer theory or post-colonialism, they will also need to carefully define their methodology (critical analyses in a cultural context) and methods.

INTERDISCIPLINARY WORK

There are areas of overlap between the research paths: Arts, Humanities and Social Sciences. A feminist literary criticism-based Ph.D., for example, might well cut across Social Science Ph.D.s, say, in interviewing some subjects, and this results in analysis of literary and creative texts and images, pulling the whole into an analytical, critical piece using the discourse of both subjects areas. One of our main tasks with Arts and Humanities students is to require that they are, indeed, explicit about approaches they are taking and about their analytical and critical framework and practices, or they might well be descriptive and celebratory but not critically focused in a dialogue with other work in the field (as with Social Science).

CREATIVE AND PERFORMING ARTS

While the supervisory processes for supervising a Creative and Performing Arts Ph.D. might be very similar to those for a Social Science or Humanities Ph.D., there are many moments where they might not be so similar. Students involved in developing creative projects tend to engage with emotions and identity in their work, to be expected to develop a creative project along with the accompanying analytical discussion of the ways in which that project, that process or product addresses the question that they are asking or issue they are exploring. The supervisor is involved in supervising both the process/product of the creative work and the writing about this work into a conventional enough Ph.D. format. It could be useful to ask students to:

- develop a reflective journal of the decisions they make in their creative work, and in their writing analytically about that work;
- try to disentangle and separate out the often intuitive, imaginative, creative work from the analytical writing that can explore and explain it to themselves and others.

SOME STUDENT EXPECTATIONS

Phillips and Pugh (1994) suggest that having the insider knowledge of student experience can help shape successful supervisor/student relationships. According to them, some of the expectations students have of you include (headings from Phillips and Pugh, comments my own):

1   *Students expect to be supervised* – some students feel left alone too much, and need guidance in terms of conceptual levels of work, as well as the actual process of the research, institutional requirement and presentation. Sometimes this feeling of being under-supervised arises from an excess of student expectation over supervisor availability. You do not have the hours to work with them side by side, and also you feel they need to develop independence and autonomy if they are to be successful researchers. See below for some suggestions on balancing guidance and autonomy, and on agreeing on manageable workloads and interactions to overcome the problems of the under-supervised student (or one who misguidedly feels they should be very closely dictated to and regulated).

2   *Students expect supervisors to read their work well in advance* – setting up good habits of working together – sending in chapters, questions, drafts in advance and developing agendas for working with the writing – will help the process.

3   *Students expect their supervisors to be available when needed* – providing clear, agreed times to meet or be in touch, being careful of boundaries so that students do not take too much of your time, and being available for pressing issues and emergencies are all important here.

4   *Students expect their supervisors to be friendly, open and supportive* – all teaching expects us to develop behaviours or performances we might be unaccustomed to or which are not naturally part of our everyday behaviour – you might be quite a retiring person yourself but for your student you will need to behave in an accessible, supportive and friendly way so that students feel they can ask questions, share difficulties and work with you. Being over friendly can get in the way of the professional expectations and behaviours, and being accessible at all times will eat into your own research and teaching time – so developing ground rules, boundaries, being there for emergencies, being personable and welcoming but focused, will help your students to advance their work and feel they can be autonomous, with a safety net provided by you.

5   *Students expect their supervisors to be constructively critical* – this is part of the process by which we help students to develop conceptually, cognitively and critically – see below about asking problematising questions that open up thought and discussion. Being restrictively critical can shut a student's work down – try: 'Had you thought of . . .?', 'Please express why you . . .', 'How else might . . . ?', rather than 'This just doesn't work', 'No!!! this won't do' and other such paralysing negative comments!

6   *Students expect their supervisors to have a good knowledge of the research area* – this is another continuum. You need to have enough specialism in the area to feel confident that you can put important literature their way, engage in fundamental discussions, provide some key to the theories and practices of the area, and comment when there are wrong directions and misunderstandings. However, in the end, your student will be more of an expert in this particular, specific area than you will, and you can supervise in a team with others who have subject specialism, if your own specialism is more focused on methodology and methods more generally rather than on the subject specifics.

7   *Students expect their supervisor to structure the tutorial or supervision session so that it is relatively easy to examine ideas* – drawing up agendas and engaging in critical, constructive discussion is examined below. The structure of the tutorial or supervision and the flow of your discussions is actually a mutual responsibility, as in all human interactions, but the fact that (however unused you might feel to this position) you are an authority figure in this relationship and do have the actual power, means that negotiating ways of working, moving on, summarising at the end, i.e. structured supervisions, are ultimately your responsibility to manage.

8   *Students expect supervisors to have sufficient interest in their research to give or direct the student to more information and links* – this is also a continuum, with you doing all the work at one end (not advisable – it is their project) and the students floundering without support at the other. If you are a subject or methodology and methods expert, you will be able and expected to digest the reading of many relevant items and share this in discussion. But if you do all the photocopying and searching yourself, then you are actually doing the research yourself, and your students could end up spoon-fed and unable to go about this research for themselves in the future. A balance is necessary. Sometimes it is possible to also put them in touch with others in the academic community who will (to a limited extent) share their knowledge and contacts and information.

9   *Students expect supervisors to be sufficiently involved in their success to help them to get a good job at the end of it all!* – of course – the Master's or Ph.D. is a step towards a career for many students and you will be asked to provide references and can suggest jobs to apply for if you come across them. However, in most instances, the Ph.D. is not an apprenticeship, and being realistic is safest, since many of us are not in a position to actually provide a job for our students – so putting people in touch, discussing possible directions and writing references are ways we can help our students. That said, you might see adverts in emails to forward or hear of others in your university and elsewhere who are looking for a good researcher/teacher, and suggesting your students apply for these jobs is helping them along in their academic career.

STAGES IN SUPERVISING POSTGRADUATES

Before you both begin:

How do your students find you? – Does the university have a website that advertises specialisms, so they might have sought you out through the website? Or have you been recommended to them, have they been allocated to you, did they answer an advertisement to undertake a specific research project in your team or individually with you? Are they one of your undergraduates? A colleague? A friend? Did they come to you by word of mouth? If you are seeking a postgraduate student to work with, you might consider all of these as ways of attracting one or more to work with you if you have specific projects in mind. Often they appear out of the blue or following the website, word of mouth, etc., and then part of your task is to ensure that your area of expertise is in alignment with

157

theirs to begin with. It does not have to be directly and absolutely in alignment, but you should have some specialist knowledge and experience in the research subject area and the methodology and methods the student wishes to use. Student expectations and their likelihood of working autonomously are, to some extent, affected by whether they have, at one extreme, applied to undertake a project you have devised, and, at the other, appeared with their own idea. Either way, you will need to shape a manageable Master's or Ph.D. out of the area. If you wish to encourage postgraduate students to work with you, you might well find that developing your own external credibility in your subject area, through publications, conferences, presentations, successful research project outcomes, applying for research grants to fund a studentship, 'growing your own' through nurturing undergraduate research skills and aspirations towards postgraduate work, all help.

Are you and the university ready? – The academic research climate is very important for students' success. Find out if there is a research development programme they can join, and what skills development it offers, what other courses, such as the use of the Statistical Package for the Social Sciences (SPSS) (for social scientists) are on offer, what the facilities are in the library, in terms of information technology and individual provisions – will they be able to have their own space to work in and their own computer or more complex, specialised hardware and software? Is there funding for field trips, research materials, conferences? Are there peer support graduate groups, seminars, postgraduate societies they can join? For international students, are there international societies and international student support? Your graduate office or school or equivalent should have the answers to some of these questions, departmental office, heads of subjects research, Students' Union, Student Services, counselling services and international office other answers. Sometimes the best source of answers is another postgraduate further along in their career.

GETTING STARTED: GUIDANCE AND AUTONOMY

One of the main issues with supervising postgraduates remains that of the delicate balance between guidance and autonomy. If we are to help empower and develop research students for a future in research, in academic life, or to transfer their research skills into the world of non-academic work, we need to ensure that they develop research skills and related generic skills and a good facility with processes, which will enable them to carry out a variety of successful tasks and both initiate ideas and solve problems, and complete projects in their future study or other work. If we over-intrude this could be disempowering, but if we fail to engage students in critical and conceptual questioning, theorising and moving successfully from the complex design of research through the management and analysis of the process and its product, findings and then through to sound presentation, we are doing them a disservice. At what point are we doing the work for them? Acting like their Mum? Over-fussing? At what point can we stand back and ensure that they are well enough prepared and focused to take the work through to fruition themselves? Ingrid Moses has developed a continuum along which supervisors and students can measure their responses to issues and ranges of guidance and autonomy. This has been refined by others, including Linda Conrad at Griffith University ('Ph.D.: Managing the Supervisory Process'), and the exercise below is built upon their work but different from it.

You might like to check with your students how far they feel they are following their responsibilities and how far they are yours as supervisor. This could be an exercise carried out individually or in a small tutorial group, and helps to bring into the open some of the issues lying behind our preconceptions, expectations and working relationships that helps:

- clarify these expectations and set misconceptions to rights;
- help to build up plans of action to ensure that the different responsibilities and actions are identified and actioned;
- prevent misunderstanding as the relationship proceeds;
- provide a sound basis for revisiting the interactions and responsibilities as the relationship develops, when and if it meets problems.

In short, this kind of exercise provides a location for discussion of interaction, something that both supervisor and students might find awkward, and particularly, perhaps, if the student comes from a learning culture that values authority, finds it difficult to question elders and those in authority, or even in the face of the well-known British politeness, which can be a real barrier to fair discussions and exchange.

Please discuss these issues and practices of responsibility and check with your student on a continuum using a scale of 1–5, where 1 is the student's responsibility and 5 that of the supervisor, asking who has the responsibility? Is it shared? How? How can good practice be established and maintained with these practices and processes?

159

ACTIVITY

Please consider the following and locate responsibility along a grid, then discuss.

Student 1 —————— Supervisor 5

Context

a   Ensuring there is an appropriate research culture into which the student can enter – e.g. support groups, peer seminars, structured modules and research activity to enable students to articulate their work and share with and support others   1 —————— 5

b   Ensuring there is sufficient and appropriate provision of technical support, e.g. computers, library support   1 —————— 5

c   Support for approaches in data analysis   1 —————— 5

d   Developing questions for the research   1 —————— 5

e   Deciding on the theoretical perspectives and key theories   1 —————— 5

f   Identifying methodology and methods   1 —————— 5

g   Designing the study and drawing up the proposal   1 —————— 5

h   Starting to deal with the literature in a dialogue and developing a voice   1 —————— 5

i   Ensuring there is a critical and conceptual level to the research from questioning givens, problematising concepts, through to analysis and findings   1 —————— 5

j   Refining note and thesis writing so that it is elegant and conveys well-expressed meaning   1 —————— 5

k   Ensuring there are both factual and conceptual conclusions   1 —————— 5

l   Ensuring coherence of the argument and the theorising throughout the dissertation/thesis   1 —————— 5

m Dealing with presentational issues such as
   number of pages, quality of the abstract, layout,
   completion   1 ————— 5

n Preparing for the viva (if there is one)   1 ————— 5

o Undertaking audits and reviews of experiments,
   etc. (post viva) and drawing up agendas for
   rewriting   1 ————— 5

p Engaging in conferences, presentation and
   publication   1 ————— 5

Discussing these areas opens up possibilities to consider:

- supervisory processes
- rights and responsibilities
- student empowerment

SUPERVISING THE RESEARCH FROM START TO FINISH, SOME KEY PRACTICES

- Establish sound working practices – this is important so that you have a framework to work to.
- Agree on well spaced out supervisions at regular intervals. These should be supported by work completed, agreed, sent and looked at in advance of the meeting – your focus is on contacts, information, reading, ideas, skills and development to suggest to your student. The student should update the research log or journal detailing what he or she has done, and queries and problems to bring up.
- Make agendas – supervisor items, student items, some short informative issues, some close work on conceptual issues or helping to develop skills, or refining wording and argument. The last item is agreeing action points and the date of the next supervision.
- Make a list of post-meeting action points for both supervisors and student (shared via email).

161

- Develop protocols.
- Agree on a range of communications – some short, sharp, quick questions or exchanges – perhaps by email, to check out an idea, send a piece of information, ask a question. Have some longer exchanges in which, as time goes on, you can provide feedback on drafts of work submitted.

RESEARCH PROCESSES

Support the student in turning an interest and a broad area into a research question – without a focus and question the student could read and gather information rather obsessively and ultimately aimlessly. The question provides a direction.

Boundaries and conceptual frameworks

Deciding on the question, conceptual framework, theoretical underpinning and methodology are all important stages in the research processes.

Students need to work out what main theories underlie their approach to the question and the ideas or concepts they are considering here, and what key theorists they know already in the field, which theories and therefore theorists they need to work on and explore further.

How will they go about their reading? Ensure they are aware that any reading of theorists and critics is in a dialogue, there are debates here, and developing a sense of the main themes, arguments, disagreements, and developments in these debates, and where the student's own work starts to fit in is essential for not only a good literature or theoretical perspectives chapter, but for the whole research enterprise – where their work is actually contributing to dialogues in the subject area rather than just summing them up.

Which methodologies? This is of major interest to Social Science students who need to carefully select methodology and methods to enable them to ask their research question. It is also important for Arts and Humanities students to be clear about approaches and methods, particularly if they are crossing boundaries, say, between producing a creative product and assessing response to it – using creative methods and perhaps interviews as a social scientist would. It is also important for them to be aware that they are taking approaches using methods in their analyses. Here, Arts and Humanities students can learn from the Social Sciences about being explicit, but they should be aware of asking those direct questions particular to the social scientist – which relate to the research practices and the methods following, i.e. asking if the work is inductive (look, ask questions, experience, see what emerges, then establish a set of arguments and beliefs, theories) or deductive (take a theory established by someone else, test it out), quantitative (data, statistical, information gathering based on the sense that the results will be reliable because there are a sufficient number of them) or qualitative (gathering response about experience, in depth, more subjective, using interviews, case studies that are valid – internally it has coherence but cannot be reliable or generalisable directly onto other work because it is too small a sample). Alternatively, both quantitative and qualitative methods can be used in a mixed method mode where appropriate to the research design.

What are the ethical implications of this work and how will they seek ethics clearance? Are they aware of the institutional ethics requirements and committees that judge their ethics? They will need to consider avoiding potential harm through being clear about withdrawing, enabling the subjects to withdraw if they are uncomfortable, not making over value judgements, keeping the names of respondents confidential, and not releasing the information to others beyond the research unless directly agreed.

Humanities and Arts students (see above) are less likely to have problems with this, but some might be mixing methods and using interviews or questionnaires, as well as undertaking a critical text based on a creative project, and ethics could be relevant.

In Arts, research students engage in focusing, questioning, cataloguing, problematising and interpreting archival material, sometimes even discovering it themselves differently, exploring how it is catalogued and critiqued. This also involves very careful and detailed charting of the works studied and a critical framework for the research and interpretation, which enables involving these resources and findings into an argument addressing a specific question.

When students are engaged in accessing specialised materials such as archives, we might well be involved in gaining access for them, as we would also help them in gaining access to sample populations of Social Science if needed.

Data collection

How will it be gathered, catalogued and analysed? If you are able to work with your student on the development of the proposal, which is the normal early stage of research, then dealing with all of these areas will form the basis of that proposal. If they already have a proposal or the basics of one is embedded with a funded project, the teasing out and clarifying of each of these stages is equally important for your students to question, problematise, identify, own and plan all those elements of their research.

Getting your student started

This is very time consuming but they do need:

- a clear research design likely to achieve a Master's dissertation or Ph.D. of quality;
- the development of agreed practices and processes of working together – meeting agendas, contracts and sharing of work will enable them to get started with the work and keep going and will also provide a sound basis for dealing with any problems that might emerge during the course of their research and in your relationship together.

Supervising the research process – an ongoing activity

An important issue here is fostering good writing habits in your students.

Good writing habits

Your students should be encouraged to start writing early on so that they engage in their own words, with their own ideas and work with the experts (the theoretical perspectives or literature reviews chapter), with the early data collection and analysis, and most particularly with the analytical, critical, conceptual level of work, with the debates in the field, and turning their own data into findings. This is essential so that they engage early on in a critical and conceptual way rather than merely a descriptive, annotating way. So, they need to move beyond:

- note taking;
- summary description;
- annotation; and
- synopsis;

to:

- problematising, setting reading and findings in debate and dialogue;
- comparison, contrasting;
- conceptualising – identifying what this might contribute to knowledge and understanding, how it might change understanding, clarify problems, raise new issues.

Your work with your students can help them in this movement through several different strategies including: critical and probing questioning, encouraging the habit of writing, and empowering your student to overcome problems.

Critical and probing questioning

This can be done either orally as you work together in a supervision, or on the text if they have written something that you would like to act both as a way of organising their thoughts and of providing some entries into the debate.

Ask your students questions such as:

- How else could this be perceived?
- What might someone else say if . . .?
- Is this all there is to say here?
- What if/what if not?
- Why does this matter?
- Does this let the way you or we use this issue . . .?
- How does your reading back up or disagree with what you have found? In what key ways?
- Which theories or theorists might be called on here to help illuminate what you have said or found? In what ways?

If you are annotating the written word, you could work on the text using track changes, which record your suggestions and their responses to those suggestions in a variety of different colours over time (someone can preserve several developing versions – or not).

Encouraging the habit of writing

This can result from asking your student to keep an annotated log of the work they carry out, their reflections on it and decision taken, discussion of how it fits into their overall work and the questions and dialogues about the area in the literature review or theoretical perspectives. It then forms part of their chapters for the Ph.D. Students fuel some of the comment they can make at the viva when asked about decisions about method, methodology, data, etc. It also helps them break any writer's block because though this is not quality complex writing as such, it is writing that feeds into their later and final drafts and their overall understanding of the research and its contribution to knowledge and debate in the field.

Empowering your student to overcome problems

There are many problems that your student could experience in their research and writing, and many students experience many of them – these include problems based on the:

- design of the research;
- the research process itself;
- level and kind of work being undertaken so that the research findings and thesis or dissertation are at a sufficiently complex, cognitive and conceptual level;
- management so that information comes in at the appropriate places in the text;
- writing, expression;
- final presentation.

Some of the problems that could be experienced about the design and process of the research include loss of samples, inability to find information and the appropriate literature, poorly constructed research design so that the research question and the methods used, such as questionnaires, interviews or critical approaches, do not yield the information and answers that they were seeking. If the research methods are not yielding the kinds of result needed, return to the question and reconsider it. Is it complex enough, does it move beyond the descriptive and accumulative to really ask critical, problematising questions of the area and provide ideas?

It is possible to ask problematising, critical and conceptual level questions at an early stage or midway into students' research in order to form or reframe their questions so that they can approach or reconsider their data. If they have only collected factual data rather than in any connected way with a specific question or problem in mind then it is possible they might have to find a way to return to their sample and ask further questions (difficult!) or to really scrutinise the data that they have and see if, when different sets of data – from questionnaires, from interviews or the literature – are compared together, some responses to the question are generated that can be suggested by some further work on, for instance, some case studies.

Some problems with writing

Some problems with writing at different stages include writing blocks. Students should develop the habit of analysing and discussing, then ensuring the clarity, coherence, structure and expression of the finished thesis or dissertation. Often there are problems working at a conceptual level rather than an accumulative level – moving up to problematising, critiquing, conceptualising data and beyond.

Completion

There is still very little literature about the expectations of examiners, and of the viva process.

Vernon Trafford and Shosh Leshem (2002) suggest students should consider the expectations and behaviours of examiners as they *begin* their research. Additionally, you, as supervisor, might find it useful to look at your *own* experience to help guide your student.

These discussions and suggestions are based on interviews with supervisors and successful doctoral candidates (2000–2004); my own experience of doctoral vivas and examination reports; the research of Trafford (2003) and of the SORTI group; workshop discussions and responses with others including Margaret Kiley (Sept. 2003) Margot Pearson (Dec. 2002), HERDSA conferences (2002, 2003), ISL (2002, 2003), EARLI (2003).

Dissertations and theses are examined by both internal and external examiners. For supervisors, the examination of students with whom we have had such a close developmental relationship seems sometimes rather like an examination of our own expertise and interactions. Of course, this is not an examination of your own work, but that of your student. However, successes and problems or failures do reflect on us, and our close emotional and professional involvement with the work means we are very concerned that a good enough dissertation or thesis actually does pass, or passes with some amendments (there are almost always amendments – in the UK only 12 per cent of Ph.D. theses go through without any real amendments).

167

✍ **ACTIVITY**

Reality check

Please consider:

What has been your experience of dissertation or thesis examining:

- as a student
- as a supervisor
- as an examiner?

What experiences, strategies issues, problems and advice have you gained from this?

List three problems:

- _____

- _____

- _____

and three strategies for examining dissertations and theses:

- _____

- _____

- _____

We need to prepare students for the examination – share with them the qualities of a good dissertation or thesis through discussing checklists such as that produced by Winter *et al.* (2000), and looking through successful theses, analysing how they have explored and been disciplined, how their work is conceptual in the abstract and operating in a well-organised, well-structured, well-expressed way throughout the thesis, ensuring that their work is coherent, original enough, publishable, organisationally sound, conceptually sound, and well expressed.

You will need to help your Master's student decide on a second internal examiner, and your Ph.D. student to choose an internal and external examiner. Choosing the right examiner is crucial, not because of the certainty involved in picking one of your friends to examine (there is no such certainty anyway!) but more to ensure that the examiners have sufficient knowledge of the field, the methodology and methods and theoretical perspectives in the research, and have enough professionalism to avoid taking out any personal or institutional grievances against your student, or acting like a prima donna and mismanaging the viva. Poor external and internal examiners are more concerned with keeping students from passing and insisting the dissertation thesis should be as perfect as they would write it (and exactly as they would write it) rather than judging it fairly on its merits and making suggestions for improvement. Good examiners give their attention to the thesis or dissertation's contribution to knowledge and conceptual levels of understanding in the subject, with the professional standards of the award in mind, and examine fairly. In vivas in the UK, the role of the internal chair is largely to keep examiners on this latter track should they wander. Note Rowena Murray's comments about examiners:

> Does the potential examiner suffer from the 'drawbridge' mentality? This is a common disease. The examiner, having achieved a higher degree, believes that he or she should be the last person to enter the ivory tower before the drawbridge is raised, and unworthy unwashed multitudes lay siege to the castle. In practice, that means that all attempts by higher degree candidates to join the elite are repulsed as below standard. The second issue relates to broadmindedness or matching. The good examiner needs either to be a user of the same broad theory and methods of data collection and analysis as the candidate, and have an interest in the empirical subject matter, or to be broadminded enough to appreciate the merits of approaches other than his or her own. It is reasonable to expect students to have a reasoned defence of their theories, methods and topic choices, both in the thesis and orally in the viva. However, it is not reasonable to ask the student to defend a school of thought against blind prejudice, if the external examiner is implacable and irrationally hostile to a position, she or he will in all likelihood not prove a fair examiner.
>
> (Murray, 2002: 146)

Murray also comments on the importance of choosing the right external in relation to the student's future, so: it is important to have an external who can write references for the next decade or so.

169

EXTERNAL EXAMINERS

The system for external examiners working with undergraduate research dissertations is similar to that of work with other undergraduate assessments – moderating internal marking, ensuring internal processes and procedures are fair and just, ensuring standards are comparable internally and externally.

The role of the external examiner in a postgraduate course at Master's level is usually similar to that for undergraduate courses – they are the second marker. The role of the external examiner on a Ph.D., Ed.D. or Pr.D. is, however, one of being first a marker of equal weight with the other marker. There could be more than one external examiner working in a team with an internal examiner.

The supervisor is the first to read through and deem as passable the thesis presented by their student but, after that, their role in the assessment process ceases, partly because the thesis has been produced in conjunction with you as supervisor so for the supervisor to be part of the final assessment would be oddly like marking some of your own work. Here are some tensions and paradoxes. The dissertation has to be handed in at the appropriate due date for a Master's course, though times of Ph.D.s might be more flexible though following the insistence in Australasia that funding for future students is dependent on postgraduates completing in three years, and ESRC and QAA rulings in the Metcalfe Report 2002. The increased expectation in the UK is that completion should be within three years. In many universities if the supervisors feel the thesis is not ready to be submitted, students can still insist on submission even if the thesis is not really ready and has flaws of structure and expression. Whether you consider it is passable or not, your reputation will be soon considered alongside the thesis even though it is your student's work. This is a professional issue of some difficulty if the result is failure or a large number of revisions. Asking students to seek an independent reviewer of the thesis, a colleague or other Ph.D. student, before submission helps to manage the process and improve the work with which you both have become far too closely involved at the final stage. Ask your student to look carefully through some successful theses right at the end and consider:

- Clarity of the abstract in identifying what the main question or questions underpinning the research are and how through carrying out the research certain conceptual as well as factual conclusions have been reached.

- Ways in which the introduction genuinely sets the scene for the question, the importance of the research and the theories and methodologies chosen, the contact, their role within this context.
- The appropriateness of the theories and debates as expressed in the theoretical perspectives or literature chapter.
- The ways in which these emerge as threads and motifs throughout the thesis, the appropriateness of methodology and methods to enable the students to ask their question, and how they are defended, set up, data produced, analysed and interpreted from them all in order to answer the question.
- How all the chapters' beginnings and endings refer back and forwards so the whole reads coherently.
- How the conclusion chapter has both factual conclusions – 'This was found . . .', 'This amount of data was found . . .' – and conceptual conclusions – 'This means that this constitutes further argument to this . . .', 'This matters because . . .'.
- The referencing is right – no references within the main texts that are not here properly in the reference or bibliography section, and vice versa, and all laid out and full enough.

The other thing to recognise is that a supervisor's work continues beyond any viva or examination result. Your Ph.D. student will probably have corrections to make when they emerge from their viva, and both Master's and Ph.D. students expect some advice on future research, work and contacts in the spirit of the collegiality of the academic community. Some of them might later (or immediately) become your own colleagues and collaborators on writing projects.

It is a very good idea to gain some practice in the role of an internal or external examiner yourself. It can help inform the supervising process, as you can advise your student what to expect from the examination. However, undertaking an external examinership is usually done for several reasons: a mix of altruism, subject interest and academic development.

A template of assessment criteria used by examiners might assist candidates in the design of research proposals and the presentation of their doctoral theses. It can also provide a framework in which candidates and their supervisors can discuss research issues 'in which both have a common interest' (Delmont *et al.*, 1998). Such a template should not be seen as a 'do-it-yourself' kit, but rather a contribution to 'demystifying the doctoral process' (Burnham, 1994; Trafford and Leshem, 2002: 31–49).

Australian universities rely on written reports rather than vivas, seeking international external examiners, typically assessing against a rating scale at one end of which is an unconditional pass, at the other a terminal fail. 'In between are several levels of suggested amendment ranging from minor amendments to a requirement to revise and resubmit the thesis for further examination' (Holbrook and Bourke, 2002b: 1). Examiner reports are usually three and a half pages long in Australia. In the UK and elsewhere there are often draft reports produced prior to a viva, and final reports according to a pro forma of varied lengths, and the result of intensive and extended engagement with a thesis (see Kiley and Mullins, 2002). After examining fifty-one examiner reports and noting the depth of much of the comment, Johnston (1997).

Supervisors and students might find it useful to pull together advice from Trafford and Leshem, Holbrook and Bourke, and Winter et al.'s definitions of a good thesis, in order to guide students in designing, beginning to write, rewriting, and finalising a successful thesis that should pass the examination. However, research conducted by Holbrook and Bourke, Trafford and Leshem, and Hartley and Fox. indicated a series of issues to do with examiner quality, consistency and transparency of criteria, hidden agendas, variation in areas covered and, in some cases, a tendency to focus on presentation to the detriment of the substantive dissertation or thesis, or on the contribution it makes to knowledge. There is a great deal of examiner variation, but the best advice to your student is to ensure that their work is at the right kind of level conceptually, well organised and argued, and well expressed and presented. This should minimise the range and kind of corrections to be made.

Kiley and Mullins (2002) and Becher (1993) report examiner reluctance to fail a thesis. However, little is yet known about the relationship between what an examiner says and the criteria against which they are examining a thesis (Pitkethly and Prosser, 1995). A small number of (non-replicable) Australian studies subjected Ph.D. examiner reports to content analysis, (Johnston, 1997; Nightingale, 1984; Pitkethly and Prosser, 1995). Shortcomings noted in examiner reports included limited disciplinary coverage, unexplicated analysis, and partial or narrow investigation of content (Holbrook and Bourke, 2002a: 3–4). Some researchers have explored how examiners differentiate between pass and fail theses, the threshold of an acceptable thesis, and outstanding theses (Holbrook and Bourke, 2002a: 4; Kiley and Mullins, 2002; Winter et al., 2000).

Holbrook and Bourke asked: 'What skills and knowledge have to be present for a candidate to pass outright, and how consistently are such

172

criteria applied? How do examiners translate the concepts of "originality, significance and contribution" into practice?' (2002a: 6).

Examiners tend to engage with a thesis as part of that dialogue in the academic community in which students themselves are engaged and some, as Johnston's (1997) research suggests, take an editorial role, operating rather like a supervisor in providing formative feedback.

Examiners react badly to a poorly written or presented thesis, which could overwhelm their judgement, blinding them to the quality of the argument and persuading them to spend their time suggesting a wealth of corrections to expression. This could be of particular concern to students for whom English is not their first language.

Holbrook and Bourke found a variety of categories of evaluative comment, some of which relate to 'communicative inaccuracies' or 'significance and contribution'. Some are summative, judgemental. Others have an instructive focus: 'formative instruction', 'instructive commentary', and 'prescription' (Holbrook and Bourke, 2002b: 8). Some examiners sum up their feelings holistically with 'this is a fine thesis'.

YOUR WORK DOES NOT END WITH THE EXAMINATION VIVA

Trafford (2003) considers a set of variables that can describe the attention paid, and the comments made, by examiners in examining theses. Some tend to comment on the presentation and construction, noting typos, etc., while at the other end of the quadrant Trafford considers conceptual levels and complexity. Comments run between the ends of the continuum and it has been noted by Trafford, and by Kiley and Mullins, that an examiner can get somewhat stuck on the presentation issues, providing advice to improve the quality of the way it is expressed, size of bar charts, length of quotations, etc., rather than on the contribution to knowledge, the originality and the conceptual, critical levels. In some respects, a successful thesis could have such relatively superficial comments since this is what needs improvement, but in other instances these comments stem from the examiners' non-engagement with the complexity of the issues discussed or other recognition that the thesis itself does not actually operate at a high enough conceptual level to warrant such discussion. The final responses and assessment of the examiner, then, can range between the conceptual clarification, expression, presentation, structural and other areas of work. Students tend to have improvements to be made to their theses since for the Ph.D. this is actually rather like submitting for

173

publication – if the thesis is acceptable enough to be seen to be able to pass, it is then dealt with as a piece of work in progress and the student is expected to improve it, whether structurally in terms of interpretation and/or conceptually, or both – at this point they will also need your support. They will also benefit from your advice and collegial support once the Ph.D. has been achieved since they will need introductions to those who can publish their research, provide them with further research funding and give them jobs.

DISCIPLINE DIFFERENCES – REVISITED: SUPERVISING SOCIAL SCIENCE POSTGRADUATE WORK

The working relationships between you and your student, outlined above, are suitable for both Social Science and Arts and Humanities research students. The main differences between the two emerge when considering the methodology, methods, and so the research in action, the ethics of work with human subjects. There might well be different rhythms to the work but this could also vary between Social Scientists and Arts or Humanities students, depending on their particular research area. These are a key issue for social scientists, because Social Science students are likely to need research methods development in the planning of appropriate questionnaires, interview schedules, focus groups, case studies, action research, ethnomethodology, phenomenology and so on. For this specific stage's needs and demands, and clarification of these, you will need to refer your student to research methods experts and to the literature that is extensive and includes: Robson (1993); Miles and Huberman (1994); Wenger and Lave (1991).

In addition to methods, they will also need to develop the appropriate skills to analyse their data. Students could well need to learn to analyse and ask questions of statistically based data and interviews and discuss thematically and in response to their research questions, and to avoid being merely detailed, narrative and descriptive but to ensure they are analytical, interpretive, provide an ethically clear framework and make conceptual conclusions.

ARTS AND HUMANITIES

Arts and Humanities students might well become inundated and accumulate a lot of data – quotations, transcripts of interviews with those providing oral histories, drafts of the development of an artefact such as a piece of music, poem, sequence, theory, creative options.

If your student were to undertake research that would result in a creative product or artefact process, as part of his or her work, then it is important to both split up the different problems of the work and ensure that the analytical, critical element of the work engages with theory-underpinning and helps to inform the creative work, which itself exemplifies and enacts an answer to, or a way of addressing, a particular research question. Some of the strategies you might undertake to begin the creative process are outlined below.

BRAINSTORM: PRODUCT/ARTEFACT VISUALISED

Engage with theory and analysis: what can this say? Whose ideas and arguments can inform it, in what ways does each element of it enable you to engage with issues and strategies about the concerns you have?

Then once the artefact has been constructed, the student needs to ask:

■ How does it engage with the conceptual and critical arguments they want to make?

You explore and express this. They will need to produce a theorised, analytical piece that engages at each stage with the critical demands and arguments they are using and shows how each element of the creative product is expressed in their point of view and argument.

In creative research work we would be involved in identifying the position and problem that the student is addressing, rather than just looking at the kind of creative, reasoned questions the student needs to ask and answer, questions such as:

■ How can white female engagement with Caribbean black culture in all forms in terms of identity and response be expressed creatively?

This and others research both a format which will help ask and answer the question in both cases, e.g. in response to the above, a student undertook a video and music project which enabled her to both talk about her engagement and to express it through choices of poetry and music, also including talking about herself and about the creative poetry and music.

175

FURTHER READING

Becher, T. (1993). 'Graduate education in Britain: the view from the ground'. In B. R. Clark (ed.) *The Research Foundations of Graduate Education: Germany, Britain, France, United States and Japan* (pp. 115–53). Berkeley, CA: University of California Press.

Conrad, L. (undated). 'Ph.D. managing the supervisory process'. Griffith University, unpublished.

Holbrook, A. (2002). 'How examiners of doctoral theses utilise the written report'. Paper presented at Examining the Quality of Doctoral Research AERA Symposium, New Orleans, 1–5 April.

—— and Bourke, S. (2002a). 'Links between research and schools: the role of postgraduate students'. *Australian Educational Researcher*, 28 (2): 15–32.

—— and —— (2002b). 'Ph.D. assessment: design of the study, qualities of examiner reports and candidature information'. Paper presented at Examining the Quality of Doctoral Research AERA Symposium, New Orleans, 1–5 April.

Johnston, S. (1997). 'Examining the examiners: an analysis of examiners' report on doctoral thesis'. *Studies in Higher Education, Journal of Higher Education*, 22 (3): 333–47.

Kiley, M. and Mullins, G. (2002). '"It's a Ph.D., not a Nobel Prize": how experienced examiners assess research theses'. *Studies in Higher Education*, 27 (4): 369–86.

Nightingale, P. (1984). 'Examination of research theses'. *Higher Education Research and Development Journal*, 3 (2): 137–50.

Phillips, E. and Pugh, D. S. (1994). *How to Get a Ph.D.: A handbook for students and their supervisors*, 2nd edn. Buckingham: Open University Press.

Pitkethly, A. and Prosser, M. (1995). 'Examiners' comments on the international context of Ph.D. theses'. In C. McNaught and K. Beattie (eds) *Research into Higher Education: Dilemmas, directions and diversions* (pp. 129–36). Melbourne: HERDSA.

Trafford, V. N. (2003). 'Questions in a doctoral vivas: views from the inside', QAA, 11 (2): 114–22. Available from: www.emeraldinsight.com/insight/viewcontentservlet?filename=published/emeraldfulltextarticle/pdf/1200 110208.pdf.

Trafford, V. N. and Leshem, S. (2002). 'Starting at the end to undertake doctoral research: predictable questions as stepping stones'. *Higher Education Review*, 35: 31–49.

Winter, R., Griffiths, M. and Green, K. (2000). 'The "academic" qualities of practice: what are the criteria for a practice-based Ph.D.?'. *Studies in Higher Education*, 25 (1): 25–37.

Chapter 11

Supervising postgraduates in the Sciences, Engineering and Medicine

In this chapter we will look specifically at the Ph.D. and focus on the aspects of supervision that are particular to Ph.D.s in Science- and Engineering-related disciplines.

DIFFERENCES BETWEEN SCIENCES AND ARTS PH.D.s

Each year about 10,000 students enter Science and Engineering Ph.D.s in the UK and about 7,000 Ph.D. students graduate each year (Roberts, 2002). In many Science and Engineering disciplines a significant proportion of these students are international students and the majority study full time.

When reviewing the differences that exist, across a university campus, in the way that Ph.D.s operate, the first aspect to consider is the initiation and starting points for the research project. It is possible to describe a continuum with the 'Arts' model at one extreme and the 'Science' model at the opposite end. In the Arts model, the project is devised by the student and it is the student who then seeks to gain funding and recruit a supervisor able to guide their work. Under the Science model, the research project is designed by the supervisor, who has (frequently) written a detailed proposal and obtained a grant to carry out the work, who then recruits a student to work on the project. The initial 'ownership' of the project is very different under the two models and this leads to very different starting points for both the project and the student/supervisor relationship (Exley and O'Malley, 1999). Many Science students are likely to follow their supervisors' clear lead at the beginning of their studies only later individualising and developing their own ideas. This transition from working more like a research assistant on the supervisor's project to

177

working more independently and picking up the ownership of their own project, needs to take place during the first twelve months of the Ph.D. in order for the student to be secure in upgrading their programme registration from M.Phil. to Ph.D. (see 'Upgrading').

A second significant difference results from the very nature of Science- and Engineering-based research. It often requires specialised equipment and research environments, which means students need to come into the university in order to carry out their work. Research in some other disciplines can be carried out anywhere where there is a networked computer, or in the library or out in the field, etc. This fundamental characteristic of Science and Engineering research means that very regular and informal contact between students and students, and supervisor(s) and students, is the norm. It also usually means that such research is often expensive in terms of resources, consumables, equipment, etc.

The cost of doing Science and Engineering research and the global competition to publish and yield results often mean that expertise becomes very focused around centres of excellence. Large research groups are more the norm and a research student is more likely to join an existing team. This means that the requirement to provide an 'active research environment' is more readily met in Science and Engineering. It also means that students have a number of people to whom they can turn for advice and guidance in addition to their supervisors. However, it can be more difficult for the students to see the coherence of their own individual project when it is a contributing segment in a much larger research activity and part of an established group effort.

Specific health and safety requirements may also affect the process of doing the research. Close supervision may be needed or the provision of specialist training, resources, equipments and safe research environments.

A final difference worth mentioning is the influence of 'industry sponsored' research in Science and, particularly, in Engineering. One example is the CASE award studentships (Collaborative Awards in Science and Engineering) in which the funding for a tightly defined project is provided by a university/industry partnership. Although the links between academia and commercial organisations do exist in other discipline areas it is often less common. In practice, sponsored projects are likely to involve both academic and industrial supervisors who will have experience of very different work cultures and have different expectations for the project and of the student. When this works well it can provide the student with a unique insight into the way research is carried out in academia and in industry. This gives students an advantage when it comes to making future career choices and can help the development of more effective academic–industrial partnerships. In the worst case scenario a student on a sponsored project might feel pulled in two very different directions by academic and industrial objectives, particularly if their work begins to yield potentially profitable and publishable results.

So, in general, Science/Engineering Ph.D. students are more likely to be part of a research group, working on an earmarked and funded research project initiated by their supervisors. They will be more likely to come to the university/institution each day and work alongside other research students and contract researchers from all over the world, particularly from South and East Asia and to be working full time on their research project.

THE CHANGING NATURE OF THE PH.D.: WHAT IS A PH.D.?

The QAA framework for HE qualifications describes a Doctorate in the following way:

Doctorates (Ph.Ds and D.Phils) are awarded to students who have demonstrated:

1) the creation and interpretation of new knowledge, through original research or other advanced scholarship, of a quality to satisfy peer review, extend the forefront of the discipline, and merit publication;

2) a systematic acquisition and understanding of a substantial body of knowledge which is at the forefront of an academic discipline or area of professional practice;

3) the general ability to conceptualise, design and implement a project for the generation of new knowledge, applications or understanding at the forefront of the discipline, and to adjust the project design in the light of unforeseen problems;

4) a detailed understanding of applicable techniques for research and advanced academic enquiry.

Typically, holders of the qualification will be able to:

a) make informed judgements on complex issues in specialist fields, often in the absence of complete data, and be able to communicate their ideas and conclusions clearly and effectively to specialist and non-specialist audiences;

b) continue to undertake pure and/or applied research and development at an advanced level, contributing substantially to the development of new techniques, ideas, or approaches;

and will have:

c) the qualities and transferable skills necessary for employment requiring the exercise of personal responsibility and largely autonomous initiative in complex and unpredictable situations, in professional or equivalent environments.

(reproduced with permission from
QAA, 2001: 14)

How much is a Ph.D. training to be a researcher and how much is it about contributing to knowledge? Many of the changes that have impacted on the Ph.D. in the UK in recent times have encouraged the viewpoint of the Ph.D. as an apprenticeship in research. The output of a Ph.D. programme is more importantly seen as being a newly trained researcher rather than the particular contribution to knowledge that the research project has resulted in. This shift in view is not unanimously held but is encouraged by the core funders of Ph.D.s and is one reason why the criterion for Ph.D.s in the UK remains 'work that is of publishable quality' rather than 'published work'. This is not the case elsewhere in the world. Students undertaking Ph.D.s in many Scandinavian countries, for example, are required to submit a thesis which is, effectively, a collection of half a dozen journal papers.

The trained researcher, however, is increasingly less likely to go on and become a career researcher or academic. More students are looking for a qualification that is more advanced than a Bachelor's or Master's degree but may not be keen to pursue an academic career path. This makes the development of the broader skills set that are associated with studying for Ph.D. even more important.

ROLES AND RESPONSIBILITIES

Supervisors can now be much clearer about their roles and responsibilities when supervising Ph.D. students as these are stipulated by universities in their own 'codes of practice' and by the Research Councils (see Box on p. 181) and other funders of research degrees.

UK RESEARCH COUNCILS

BBSRC   Biotechnology and Biological Sciences Research Council

CCLRC   Council for the Central Laboratory of the Research Councils

EPSRC   Engineering and Physical Sciences Research Council

ESRC   Economic and Social Research Council

MRC   Medical Research Council

NERC   Natural Environmental Research Council

STFC   Science and Technology Facilities Council

AHRC   Arts and Humanities Research Council

THE RESEARCH COUNCILS UK

The influence of the Research Councils on practice is very significant in Science and Engineering disciplines as a large proportion of the funding for studentships comes through them. STFC describes the two roles of a supervisor as first, being scientific stimulation, motivation and guidance and, second, ensuring the student makes good progress and submits their thesis in four years. The published guidance from STFC does strongly focus on this second aspect of supervision by saying:

The supervisor should:

- be part of a professional network of national and international colleagues;
- be aware of academic standards of research;
- ensure that a research environment is created that allows research to be conducted within the principles of good scientific practice;
- be able to assess a topic of suitable scope;
- be qualified to supervise the particular research topic;
- actively supervise the research, balancing the student's role between apprenticeship and independence;
- make it easy to exchange ideas;

181

- monitor the work and be constructively critical, creating the appropriate environment e.g. reading work in advance, maximising time in meetings with the student;
- be friendly, open and supportive;
- be accessible frequently to the students and be available when needed;
- agree on appropriate working arrangements (e.g. working hours, holidays, etc.);
- help the student develop a work plan and timetable with short term goals and milestones;
- be able to advise on conferences, short courses and the presentation of papers;
- advise on publications and agree who should be credited as first author;
- be watchful for emerging problems: academic, medical, financial, pastoral and aware of appropriate services;
- ensure the student is aware of the university's formal procedures and policies (e.g. health and safety, equal opportunities, etc.);
- assist with career development;
- advise and help students secure a job at the end of it all, remembering that many will move away from academia.

(STFC website, www.scitech.ac.uk)

To carry out such responsibilities the BBSRC suggest that a supervisor needs a range of skills. These include the skills of teaching, coaching and mentoring that involve communication, counselling, assessment and monitoring, giving feedback and helping the student to develop their own problem-solving skills.

Students, too, are given much guidance about what they can expect from their supervisors and how they can expect to work with them. However, every supervisory relationship is individual and words on a page can only communicate so much about how this process will actually work. Student expectations tend to revolve around the belief that they will be supervised and clearly guided (told what to do), and that they will have a supervisor who will have the time and commitment to read their work, give them honest and constructive feedback and be open and supportive. They also expect that the supervisor will be knowledgeable about the subject and the process of doing a Ph.D. and can help them with their career choices later on (Phillips and Pugh, 2000).

HEALTH AND SAFETY AND ETHICAL APPROVAL

In the Science and Engineering disciplines it is also worth mentioning two other aspects to be considered at the beginning of a Ph.D., the first being issues of health and safety, and the second being the possible need to gain ethical approval for a particular project.

Some research projects may require particular risk assessments to be carried out prior to work commencing, while all others will at least require the students to be familiar with departmental health and safety rules and regulations and to work within the boundaries advised. New students will need to know how to minimise the potential risk of dangerous effects from radiation, fire, biological hazards and chemical release, and they must know how to protect themselves, others and the environment from harm. The supervisor's role will be to ensure risks are properly assessed and appropriate training is undertaken if necessary. In the case of using radiation, students will also need to be regularly screened and monitored to ensure their exposure remains within safe limits.

Any research projects involving human or animal subjects must not begin until the necessary project and personal licences have been obtained along with local ethical approval. This is also the case for some other forms of scientific work. Usually the ability to give ethical approval for a project is delegated by the university to the Departmental Ethics Committee and it is the responsibility of the supervisor and the student to seek this before any work begins. In many places this process can take several months and has the potential to hold up a research project and, therefore, in some cases supervisors seek this approval even before a student begins.

THE PERFECT PROJECT BRIEF

What form of research project also provides an appropriate 'training vehicle' for a Ph.D. studentship in your discipline area? The initial project proposal needs to include at least two dimensions to enable to student to learn how to become a researcher and contribute to the understanding of their topic. This is summarised in Figure 11.1.

The thinking is that the project would include aspects that the supervisor believes are straightforward and likely to yield results so that the student can gain experience and learn how to analyse, interpret, discuss and present their findings. But if the project was so 'sure' and predictable this would be unlikely to be sufficient for a Ph.D. qualification. So the project

- ■ **Straightforward from the supervisor's perspective**
- ■ **Doable, achievable**
- ■ **Data generating**
- ■ **Confidence building**

- ■ **Less certain, more unknown, riskier from the supervisor's perspective**
- ■ **Demanding, challenging**
- ■ **Exciting**

■ FIGURE 11.1   Model of the 'perfect' project proposal

proposal would also need to include elements from the second box in the figure, which cover aspects of the project that are outside the direct control and influence of the supervisor/adviser. This could include the development of new research techniques and methodologies outside the supervisor's personal experience, the investigation of very new and unfamiliar avenues of research or the requirement to collect information from more uncertain and less reliable sources, etc. The more speculative activities in 'box 2' may well be less likely to lead immediately to results and publications but if they did it is likely that they would make a greater contribution to the field and advancement in knowledge.

The mix of these two elements, 'safety and risk', are necessary for a Ph.D. project. However, the implications of such an approach do mean that there are many excellent research projects that do not provide an appropriate training vehicle for a three (or four?) year Ph.D.

In Science and Engineering disciplines, where the initial project proposal is usually devised by the supervisor, he or she can build these factors into the research plans. However, if a student is developing the project outline, the role of the supervisor will be to counsel the student on how to build appropriate 'safety nets' into the Ph.D. project proposal. Supervisors (attending workshops) often comment that their students' initial proposals are over-ambitious and lack 'back up' plans.

SUPERVISORY MEETINGS

There are at least two kinds of meetings that take place between students and supervisors. There are the informal, drop-in, unscheduled meetings that are very important for the supervisory relationship and help communicate interest and enthusiasm. These often take place very frequently in Science and Engineering disciplines and are the heart of the process of mentoring and coaching that takes place. However, there is also a need for formal, business meetings that are scheduled and planned at appropriate intervals during the project. These may take place on a weekly, fortnightly or monthly basis depending on the project and the people. Care should be taken to provide an environment free from distraction and interruption, where both students and supervisors feel able to do and say what they need to and the outcomes of the meeting can be accurately recorded. Many universities give clear guidance on the nature and style of supervisory meetings and it is increasingly the case that a minimum number of meetings a year are stipulated. For example, at the University of Nottingham, at least ten meetings a year for full-time students, and six meetings a year for part-time students, is stipulated as a minimum entitlement.

Ph.D. advisers (e.g. postdoctoral workers who support the day-to-day work of the Ph.D. student in the laboratory) might not necessarily be included in the formal supervisory meetings and will be more reliant on informal meetings. Again it is helpful if the ways of working are agreed from the outset and reviewed as the project proceeds. How are all parties to be kept 'in the loop' and coordination between members of the broader supervisory team to be achieved?

Recording and documenting the agreements and outcomes of business meetings is strongly recommended by the QAA Code of Practice (Precept 15). This is considered to be good practice because it allows both student and supervisor(s) to be clear about what needs to be done and how it will happen. It also provides an audit trail that describes the student's progress and that can be reviewed by the supervisory team. The meeting record can also provide evidence of how the supervision was conducted.

185

This could be important if ever a student (or a supervisor) had reason to lodge a complaint about their experiences. Although this is very rare, there are a small number of students who are dissatisfied with their Ph.D. supervision and cases do sometimes end in formal complaints and appeals procedures. In extremely rare circumstances a student might even seek legal redress.

Some universities and departments have a standardised protocol for recording supervisory meetings with records being held centrally in departmental offices. However, in many institutions the method of recording meetings is left to the individual supervisor and student. Using email is very popular and efficient. For example, the student would be asked to send a brief email message to their supervisor the day after the meeting. The message should include the outcomes of the meeting and document any actions agreed. The message may also usefully include time and date of the next formal meeting and future plans. The supervisor would respond to this email with any changes or additions. This communication is dated and held on the university server, thus providing an accurate record of the exchange.

Such an approach has many benefits. The student retains ownership of the project; the supervisors have an efficient system in place that allows them to have a final input into the documented outcomes of a meeting and co-supervisors/advisers and/or the departmental postgraduate tutor can very easily be copied into the email exchange, thus generating a centralised record of supervision, which can be monitored if appropriate.

There are, however, a number of systems of 'keeping a record' that supervisors use. Some supervisors like to keep a handwritten note that both student and supervisor sign at the end of the meeting before photocopying it so both can keep a copy. Some use a standard, carbon copier pro forma for recording supervisory meetings (see an example in Figure 11.2). Others prefer to write up notes after the meeting and sign and exchange them later. The choice depends on personal style and context.

Many students are now using their own PDP protocols and files. These usually include meeting record pro formas. However, supervisors must remember that PDPs are owned by the student and do not necessarily provide the 'evidence' of supervision that the supervisor would wish to hold. A final comment relates to the Freedom of Information Act, which means that all information held on students should be accessible to that student. So it is important that any record or document held is agreed and available for the student to see.

SUPERVISORY MEETING RECORD SHEET

Date   _____

Supervisor(s)   _____

Student   _____

Time (start)   _____

Time (end)   _____

Summary of activities since last meeting

_____

_____

_____

Agenda items for discussion

(e.g. decisions that need to be made, agreement of research plans, points where feedback is sought, etc.)

_____

_____

_____

Comments (Supervisor)

_____

_____

_____

Comments (Student)

_____

_____

_____

Agreed plans (actions and decisions)

(e.g. who does what by when?)

_____

_____

_____

Signed (Supervisor)   _____

Signed (Student)   _____

Date of next meeting   _____

FIGURE 11.2   An example of a pro forma to record the process and outcomes of a formal supervisory meeting

SUPERVISORY TEAMS

Supervisory teams have been more usually the case in Science but now are encouraged for all disciplines.

A student working with a supervisor was very much the normal mode of Ph.D. study twenty years ago. This placed a huge burden of responsibility on the supervisor and meant that the student only had easy access to one person's skills, knowledge, experience and perspective. In more recent times the Research Councils that support work in Science and Engineering disciplines, have been keen to encourage the notion of joint supervision and support through supervisory teams as the norm. The QAA in their code of practice also encourage the establishment of supervisory teams, seeing them as an excellent way of providing a broader base of guidance with the added benefit of 'in built' safety nets, i.e. if the main supervisor were to leave or there was a breakdown in the student–supervisor relationship other members of the team could step in and provide some consistency of care.

The benefits of supervisory teams are clear in principle but in practice co-supervision can lead to difficulties for all involved if roles and responsibilities are not clearly defined and agreed upfront. The student can potentially fall between supervisors and problems can be undetected. It is therefore crucial that a primary supervisor is identified and the nature of the supportive roles played by other supervisors is described at the beginning of the project.

Many universities require new supervisors to work with an experienced supervisor until they have gained some experience themselves. Institutions usually require that a novice supervisor has worked with one (or maybe more) student through to completion before they are allowed to act as a primary supervisor. Working with an established and more senior colleague, the new supervisor has the opportunity to share concerns, observe practice and discuss approach as they develop their own way of supervising. However, as with the supervisory arrangement, this 'mentoring' arrangement also needs to be specified and agreed upfront. It can save later confusion and potential bad feeling if the details of how the co-supervision is going to be conducted is agreed and documented at the beginning of the process.

OVERSEEING TRAINING

The Research Councils have played an important role in setting standards and identifying good practice in the provision of skills training for research students. A Joint Skills Statement (see pp. 190–2) has now been agreed and sets out the skills that a doctoral research student would be expected to master during their Ph.D. This has greatly assisted universities in developing wide-ranging skills training programmes for research students aimed at ensuring students not only gain specific research skills and techniques but wider employment-related skills.

The Research Councils do expect that there will be additional requirements depending on the particular discipline but the Joint Skills Statement does provide a standard by which students can monitor their own development and supervisors can assess the particular needs of individual students.

In general, skills training is provided through five complementary routes:

- by the supervisor(s) and the supervisory team;
- by the department, school or faculty;
- by the university/institution (e.g. by University Graduate Schools, Staff Development Units and Academic Registry);
- by the funder (e.g. Research Council, charity, sponsoring body, industrial partner);
- by external agencies (e.g. UK Grad).

Supervisors might only be involved in providing a small proportion of the training directly but they oversee all of it. They help the student to identify their needs, access provision and review their learning. To do this the supervisor(s) will need to assess their student's abilities and monitor their skills development both formally and informally. However, the real challenge is in encouraging and supporting students to do this for themselves as they move towards becoming independent researchers.

In Science and Engineering disciplines much of the 'hands-on research technique and methods' training is provided very locally and may involve coaching from other Ph.D. students and contract research staff working in the department or school. Research technicians frequently provide input and guidance as Ph.D. students learn how to use equipment and develop practical skills. Other academics often share their particular expertise and specialisms willingly with research students and provide access to very advanced and tailored training on a one-to-one basis.

Schools and faculties provide research methodology courses and discipline-based training routes. While University Graduate Schools increasingly provide generic skills training in written and oral communication,

THE JOINT SKILLS STATEMENT

The skills training requirements identified by the Research Councils
www.bbsrc.ac.uk/funding/training/skill_train_req.pdf.

A) Research skills and techniques – to be able to demonstrate:

- The ability to recognise and validate problems
- Original, independent and critical thinking, and the ability to develop theoretical concepts
- A knowledge of recent advances within one's field and in related areas
- An understanding of relevant research methodologies and techniques and their appropriate application within one's research field
- The ability to critically analyse and evaluate one's findings and those of others
- An ability to summarise, document, report and reflect on progress

B) Research environment – to be able to:

- Show a broad understanding of the context, at the national and international level, in which research takes place
- Demonstrate awareness of issues relating to the rights of other researchers, of research subjects, and of others who may be affected by the research, e.g. confidentiality, ethical issues, attribution, copyright, malpractice, ownership of data and the requirements of the Data Protection Act
- Demonstrate appreciation of standards of good research practice in their institution and/or discipline
- Understand relevant health and safety issues and demonstrate responsible working practices
- Understand the processes for funding and evaluation of research
- Justify the principles and experimental techniques used in one's own research
- Understand the process of academic or commercial exploitation of research results

C) Research management – to be able to:

- Apply effective project management through the setting of research goals, intermediate milestones and prioritisation of activities
- Design and execute systems for the acquisition and collation of information through the effective use of appropriate resources and equipment
- Identify and access appropriate bibliographical resources, archives, and other sources of relevant information
- Use information technology appropriately for database management, recording and presenting information

D) Personal effectiveness – to be able to:

- Demonstrate a willingness and ability to learn and acquire knowledge
- Be creative, innovative and original in one's approach to research
- Demonstrate flexibility and open-mindedness
- Demonstrate self-awareness and the ability to identify own training needs
- Demonstrate self-discipline, motivation, and thoroughness
- Recognise boundaries and draw upon/use sources of support as appropriate
- Show initiative, work independently and be self-reliant

E) Communication skills – to be able to:

- Write clearly and in a style appropriate to purpose, e.g. progress reports, published documents, thesis
- Construct coherent arguments and articulate ideas clearly to a range of audiences, formally and informally through a variety of techniques
- Constructively defend research outcomes at seminars and viva examination
- Contribute to promoting the public understanding of one's research field
- Effectively support the learning of others when involved in teaching, mentoring or demonstrating activities

F) Networking and teamworking – to be able to:

- Develop and maintain co-operative networks and working relationships with supervisors, colleagues and peers, within the institution and the wider research community
- Understand one's behaviours and impact on others when working in and contributing to the success of formal and informal teams
- Listen, give and receive feedback and respond perceptively to others

G) Career management – to be able to:

- Appreciate the need for and show commitment to continued professional development
- Take ownership for and manage one's career progression, set realistic and achievable career goals, and identify and develop ways to improve employability
- Demonstrate an insight into the transferable nature of research skills to other work environments and the range of career opportunities within and outside academia
- Present one's skills, personal attributes and experiences through effective CVs, applications and interviews

teaching and learning, preparing for assessment, etc., funders and external agencies such as UK Grad, specialise in providing professional and employment skills, often helping to raise awareness of opportunities and encouraging career planning.

> Doctoral researchers are our most talented: they have the potential to make a significant difference to the economic competitiveness of the UK. The UK GRAD Programme has a key role in enabling them to realise their potential.
>
> (UK Grad www.grad.ac.uk/cms/ShowPage/
> Home_page/About_us/Introduction/p!eeXdbla)

The supervisor is uniquely placed to steer the student through the complex array of training provision and to make sure that training is appropriate and timely for the student.

It is important to stress that training and development are not just about going on courses and attending workshops. The vast majority of development takes place through less formalised experiences such as observing colleagues and by regular engagement and participation in departmental activities such as 'journal clubs' and 'research seminar programmes'.

Logging and reflecting upon training is core to the use of student PDR (Personal Development Record) and again students may need guidance and encouragement from their supervisors to do this. The PDR might contain a section such as this:

Reflective journal – training needs

Please include actions taken to meet your identified learning and skills development needs, e.g.:

- What were the key learning points from your training activities?
- Highlight your achievements.
- Show your plans.
- What strengths, weaknesses, opportunities and problems have you identified this year?
- What are your targets for next year and how are you going to meet these?

Although some new Ph.D. students will have experience of producing records of achievement and reflective logs before, many will not and need guidance and encouragement to do so.

MONITORING PROGRESS: INSTITUTIONAL SYSTEMS

The formalised staging posts for a Ph.D. research degree vary from one institution to another, however, a suggested generic scheme is given in Box 11.1.

Students who have a Master's degree may be permitted to register directly for a Ph.D. degree but the majority of students in the UK are initially admitted to read for the degree of M.Phil., with the expectation that this will be upgraded to a Ph.D. registration when they have demonstrated satisfactory progress. In some institutions this pre-upgrade time is referred to as the probationary period. Upgrade procedures vary in time

BOX 11.1 MONITORING A Ph.D.

Typical review stages for a full-time student

6-month review

To assess a new student's initial progress and the suitability of the selected research topic and methodology.

9-month review

Particularly important for students whose initial progress is causing some concern (this is because the institutional student return to government will consider students who have been on a research programme for 12 months to be registered Ph.D. students and include them in completion statistics).

First-year review

The student will have prepared a report or paper on their progress to date, literature review, choice of methodologies and plans for future work. The student is usually asked to present their report to a Progress Review Committee (PRC) and members of the committee will question the student and offer constructive criticism of the project. The PRC may set progress targets if appropriate or necessary. If the students have been initially registered as M.Phil. students and they wish to upgrade their registration to that of Ph.D., the first-year review may be referred to as the transfer or upgrade report and viva.

18-month review

For those students who gave cause for concern at the end of their first year to check that targets are being met and progress is adequate.

Second- and third-year reviews

The PRC will meet with the student at the end of each year and consider a short updating and planning report from the student.

and format but usually take place towards the end of the first year and include the submission of a significant piece of written report and the oral presentation of work, which could take place in a viva, a presentation to a research committee and/or, more commonly, through presenting a departmental seminar. Some universities also require research students to have achieved taught course credits (e.g. 20 credits) from the Research

Training Programme before they can upgrade. Others might wish to see evidence that a student has made appropriate progress and has clear plans for completion, yet others wish to see a detailed literature review and research plan. Upgrade is, therefore, a very important aspect of any monitoring system.

MONITORING SUPERVISION

Institutions are required to monitor supervision and do so through a mix of questionnaires and interviews with both students and supervisors. This is usually done on an annual basis with all parties being asked to comment on the effectiveness of the supervisory relationship and to bring any difficulties to light. In extreme circumstances it is possible to change supervisors, or have an additional supervisor appointed, because of a breakdown in the supervisory relationship and the occurrence of serious conflicts between student and supervisor. In reality this is not at all ideal as there might be difficulty in locating another person who has the appropriate expertise to supervise the project. It is therefore often the last resort for a Ph.D. student who is not progressing with their original supervisor. For the majority of students and supervisors monitoring is no more than a routine check and gives an opportunity to nip little problems in the bud or request small changes in supervision arrangements.

PRESENTING, WRITING AND PUBLISHING

In Science and Engineering disciplines, supervisors are likely to strongly encourage their students to present their work at conference and to publish their findings in refereed journals. Learning how to take your work out to the wider research community is part of the training afforded by a Research Degree Programme (RDP).

Through conversation with supervisors in the Science and Engineering disciplines it is clear that the norm is for students to first present their work at a departmental or school seminar, then to progress to a national or international conference or meeting to present their research as a poster or in a talk. Supervisors are usually very involved in helping their students to present their work, frequently feeling that the quality of what and how a student presents reflects upon them as supervisors. Helping students to structure their thoughts and material, consider the needs and interests of their audience and practise their skills of presentation through rehearsal, are all supervisory roles. Attending your student's departmental seminar and de-briefing with them afterwards are obvious ways you can help. Trying to give some focus to 'how' they presented as well as 'what' was said, is important to build confidence. Most students are nervous about presenting, especially when it comes to answering questions from the floor. Discussing likely question areas and sharing tactics with them for handling the difficult or unexpected question will help here. For example, asking the person to repeat the question to give a little thinking time, taking two or three questions together and answering them in a preferred order and saying 'good question, I hadn't thought of that before, do you have any views on that?' if you have no idea, etc.

Because of the nature of project initiation in the Sciences (i.e. supervisors frequently provide the initial project brief) it is common practice for supervisors to co-author papers with their students, but it is also true that detailed publishing practices do vary significantly. Often on a discipline-by-discipline basis expectations vary. What are the cultural norms for your discipline? Does the supervisor usually go first or last in a list of authors; who should be named corresponding author; and how will co-authorship actually work in practice? Agreeing the order of authors on a paper, even before a word has been written, is a good basic principle.

This variation also extends to expectations about the likely number of papers a student will be able to write during their Ph.D. In some fast-moving fields, the 'publish or perish' adage rings very true and supervisors will encourage students to write shorter papers more frequently. This may produce several papers while in other fields one longer paper might be the norm. It is very unusual for Science and Engineering theses to be turned into published books (this can happen in the Arts disciplines). However, it may be possible for the thesis to be produced as a series of bound papers. This is likely to be a route only open to staff Ph.D. candidates in the UK but is the norm in many Scandinavian countries.

Writing frequently during the Ph.D. will help the student enormously when it comes to writing their thesis, whether it be journal papers, reports or just keeping good notes and research logs. In Science and Engineering many departments demand that research logs are kept in an organised and transparent way so that experiments can be accurately repeated and intellectual property appropriately recognised. Through gaining early sight of a student's writing a supervisor can gauge the amount of support he or she needs and can organise appropriate additional help and training if necessary. This is best done early in the Ph.D. and not when the thesis is being written. A discussion with the student on the nature of feedback you aim to give can be very helpful too, especially when considering that a book proofreader will often read a text three times, first to check for meaning, second to check for structure and organisation and, third, to check for the technicalities of language, spelling and grammar, etc. What is a supervisor aiming to give feedback on? Will he or she correct spelling mistakes or are they reading work for style, consistency, scientific accuracy, checking data or statistics, etc.? Again, there are no rules but it is important that a student understands what has been looked at (and what hasn't) and does not assume that the supervisor is a complete quality control system.

SUPPORTING THE FINAL STAGES: WRITING AND PRODUCING A THESIS

Writing a thesis is a once in a life-time occupation and most students need lots of help and guidance from their supervisor(s) at this time in their Ph.D. programme. Planning and time management are key. It is helpful if a student can approach the task of thesis production with a clear and costed plan, where the cost is fundamentally their and their supervisors' time. All the supervisors consulted say that writing the thesis always takes longer than their students expected. Guides suggest allocating at least six months to the primary task of writing and editing the thesis but student and supervisor(s) need to sit down and map out a realistic plan that takes into account the time it takes getting and responding to feedback and proofreading and checking final copy.

A sensible starting point is to ask the student to outline the sections or chapters of the thesis, highlighting the main arguments and contribution to knowledge being made. The importance of how having a view of what the final product will look like and being clear from the outset which are the really important issues to address and points to make can help the student focus has been stressed by Tailor and Beasley (2004). Many students do struggle with the writing-up phase of their Ph.D. Writer's block, loss of motivation and feelings of inadequacy are reasonably commonplace and supervisors need to be aware that students who have become very competent and effective researchers can lose their way when it comes to pulling a thesis together. Maybe this is even more the case in Science and Engineering disciplines when students have been drawn to ways of studying and conducting research that usually require active experimentation, learning through doing and even physical activity. The realisation that a student, who has begun to work quite independently, needs additional support again, can take supervisors by surprise.

197

A thesis can have a number of structures but in Science and Engineering a common form is:

- introduction and literature review;
- materials and methods;
- substantive results sections (results and analysis);
- discussion (maybe a separate chapter or included at the end of each results chapter);
- conclusions and future directions.

Many students begin by writing materials and methods chapters or key results chapters, leaving introduction and discussion chapters till the end. But there is no rule and if the student has produced a detailed literature review for their upgrade or first-year report then this may be a good place to begin to produce the thesis. In essence, good advice seems to be 'start writing where you think it is easiest'.

If students do get stuck a supervisor can suggest a number of strategies that they can try:

- Write for five minutes or 'free writing'. To set a stopwatch and just write down whatever comes into their heads. Don't stop and check things just write as much as you can in the time – fill the page. This makes a separation between creativity and editing that can be very helpful.
- Use mind mapping to help lateral thinking and see ways of linking ideas and themes together.
- Write short paragraphs on main ideas, print them off and physically move them about to find a sensible ordering and logical flow.
- Take regular breaks and reward themselves with treats, such as a day off or a bar of chocolate, for achieving writing goals.

It may also help to ask to see small pieces of writing quite frequently to help set useful external goals and use the giving of constructive and encouraging feedback to motivate. If there are other students writing up at the same time in the department a supervisor could encourage the establishment of a writing buddy system in which students swap draft work and give each other feedback and suggestions before handing work in to the supervisor. Also asking students who else can help them proofread and check their editing is useful. A colleague, friend or partner outside the discipline can often provide invaluable help in these final checking stages.

FURTHER READING

Engineering and Physical Sciences Research Council (EPSRC) (1997) *Research Student and Supervisor: An approach to good supervisory practice.* Swindon: Engineering and Physical Science Research Council.

Exley, K. and O'Malley, C. (1999). 'Supervising Ph.D.s in science and engineering'. In G. Wisker and N. Sutcliffe, *Good Practice in Postgraduate Supervision* (pp. 39–56). SEDA Paper 106. Birmingham: SEDA.

Quality Assurance Agency for Higher Education (QAA) (2004). 'Code of practice for the assurance of academic quality and standards in HE: Postgraduate research programmes'. Available from: www.qaa.ac.uk/academic infrastructure/codeOfPractice/default.asp. Accessed 2 November 2007.

USEFUL WEBSITES

British Academy: www.britac.ac.uk/. Accessed 2 November 2007.

The Biotechnology and Biological Sciences Research Council (BBSRC): www. bbsrc.ac.uk/. Accessed 2 November 2007.

Engineering and Physical Sciences Research Council (EPSRC): www.epsrc. ac.uk/default.htm. Accessed 2 November 2007.

Gateway on Research Supervision

The 'Gateway on Research Supervision' provides links to websites offering information, advice and support useful for new supervisors and others involved in supervising and training.

Medical Research Council: www.mrc.ac.uk/index.htm. Accessed 2 November 2007.

The Natural Environment Research Council: www.nerc.ac.uk/. Accessed 2 November 2007.

Science and Technology Facilities Council: www.scitech.ac.uk/. Accessed 2 November 2007.

Particle Physics and Astronomy Research Council (now the Science and Technology Facilities Council) (1996). *An Approach to Good Supervisory Practice for Supervisors and Research Students.* Swindon: Particle Physics and Astronomy Research Council.

The Royal Society: www.royalsoc.ac.uk/. Accessed 2 November 2007.

Universities UK: www.universitiesuk.ac.uk/. Accessed 2 November 2007.

—— (no date) 'A concordat on contract research staff career management'. Available from: www.universitiesuk.ac.uk/activities/RCIdownloads/ rciconcordat.pdf. Accessed 2 November 2007.

Bibliography

Ashwin, P. (2005). 'Variations in students' experiences of the "Oxford Tutorial"'. *HE*, 50 (4), 631–44.

Atherton, T. (1999). *How to Be Better at Delegation and Coaching*. London: Kogan Page.

Band, S. and Parker, A. (2002). 'Ethnic minority undergraduate scheme (EMUS): post mentoring research'. National Mentoring Consortium, University of East London. Available from www.uel.ac.uk/nmc/mentoring/index.htm. Accessed 25 September 2007.

Bartlett, A., May, M. and Holzknecht, S. (1994). 'Discipline-specific academic skills at postgraduate level: a model'. In K. Channock (ed.) with V. Burley, *Integrating the Teaching of Academic Discourse into Courses in the Disciplines* (pp. 284–7). Melbourne: Language and Academic Skills Units of La Trobe University.

Baume, D. (2003). 'Managing environments for portfolio-based reflective learning (MEPRL) – goal sharpening'. University of Newcastle: www.eportfolios. ac.uk.

Becher, T. (1993). 'Graduate education in Britain: the view from the ground'. In B. R. Clark (ed.) *The Research Foundations of Graduate Education: Germany, Britain, France, United States, Japan* (pp. 115–53). Berkeley, CA: University of California Press.

Becker, L. (2003). *How to Manage Your Arts, Humanities and Social Science Degree*. London: Palgrave.

Bierema, L. and Hill, J. (2005). 'Virtual mentoring and HRD'. *Advances in Developing Human Resources*, 7 (4): 556–68.

Biggs, J. B. (1978). 'Individual and group differences in study processes and the quality of learning outcomes'. *British Journal of Educational Psychology*, 48: 266–79.

—— (ed.) (1991). *Teaching for Learning: The view from cognitive psychology*. Hawthorn, Vic.: ACER.

—— and Rihn, B. A. (1984). 'The effects of intervention on deep and surface approaches to learning'. In J. R. Kirby (ed.), *Cognitive Strategies and Educational Performance* (pp. 279–93). London: Academic Press.

Boud, D. (1995). *Enhancing Learning through Self Assessment*. London: Kogan Page.

—— (2001). 'Creating a work-based curriculum'. In D. Boud and N. Solomon (eds) *Work-Based Learning: A new higher education?*. Buckingham: SRHE/Open University Press.

Bourner, T. and Barlow, J. (1991). *The Student Induction Handbook*. London: Kogan Page.

Brandon, D. and Payne, J. (2002). 'Breakdown'. In N. Stanley and J. Manthorpe (eds) *Students' Mental Health Needs*. London: Jessica Kingsley.

Brockbank, A. and McGill, I. (2006). *Facilitating Reflective Learning through Mentoring & Coaching*. London: Kogan Page.

Brockett, R. and Hiemstra, R. (1991). *Self-Direction in Adult Learning: Perspectives on theory, research and practice*. London and New York: Routledge.

Brookfield, S. (ed.) (1986). *Self-Directed Learning: From theory to practice* (*New Directions for Continuing Education* 25). San Francisco, CA: Jossey-Bass.

Brown, G. (2004). *How Students Learn*. London: RoutledgeFalmer.

Burkitt, I., Husband, C., Mackenzie, J., Torn, A. and Crow, R. (2001). *Nurse Education and Communities of Practice*. London: ENB.

Burnham, P. (1994). 'Surviving the viva: unravelling the mysteries of the Ph.D. oral'. *Journal of Graduate Education*, 1: 30–4.

Capstick, S. (2004). 'Benefits and shortcomings of peer-assisted learning (PAL) in higher education: an appraisal by students'. Paper prepared for the Peer Assisted Learning Conference at Bournemouth University, January 2004. Available from: www.peerlearning.ac.uk/pal_conference_2004.html (revised versions of these conference papers may have been published since).

Cargill, M. (1996). 'An integrated bridging program for international post-graduate students'. *Higher Education Research and Development*, 15 (2): 177–88.

Coe, S. (2004). 'Exploring a personal experience of coaching'. Available from www.business.heacademy.ac.uk/resources/reflect/conf/2004/coe/index.html. Accessed 3 April 2006.

Collishaw, S., Maughan, B., Goodman, R. and Pickles, A. (2004). 'Time trends in adolescent mental health'. *A Journal of Child Psychology and Psychiatry*, 45 (8): 1350–62.

Committee of Vice-Chancellors and Principals of the Universities of the United Kingdom (2000). *Guidelines on Student Mental Health Policies and Procedures for Higher Education Universities*. London: Committee of Vice-Chancellors and Principals of the Universities of the United Kingdom.

Conrad, L. (Ongoing). 'Managing the supervisory process'. Ph.D. thesis. Griffith University, unpublished.

Cottrell, S. (2001). *Teaching Study Skills and Supporting Learning*. Basingstoke: Palgrave.

—— (2003). *The Study Skills Handbook*. Basingstoke: Palgrave Macmillan.

Cox, E. (2003). 'The contextual imperative: implications for coaching and mentoring.' *International Journal of Evidence Based Coaching and Mentoring*, 1 (1): 9–22.

Cropper, A. (2000). 'Mentoring as an inclusive device for the excluded: black students' experience of a mentoring scheme'. *Social Work Education*, 19 (6): 597–607.

Cryer, P. (1997). *Handling Common Dilemmas in Supervision: Guide no. 2. Issues in postgraduate supervision, teaching and management*. London: Society for Research into Higher Education and the *Times Higher Education Supplement*.

Davies, S., Swinburne, D. and Williams, G. (2006). *Writing Matters: The Royal Literary Fund report on student writing in higher education*. London: The Royal Literary Fund.

Dearing, R. (1997). *The National Committee of Inquiry into Higher Education*. Available from www.leeds.ac.uk/educol/ncihe/. Accessed 22 August 2007.

Delamont, S., Parry, O. and Atkinson, P. (1998). 'Creating a delicate balance: the doctoral supervisor's dilemma'. *Teaching in Higher Education*, 3 (2): 157–72.

Dewey, J. (1963). *Experience and Education*. New York: Collier.

DfES (2003a). *The Future of Higher Education*. London: DfES.

—— (2003b). *Widening Participation*. London: DfES.

Dinitz, S. (2004). 'Assessment of "Exploring the potential of peer tutoring in developing student writing" project'. Higher Education Academy English Subject Centre. Available from www.english.heacademy.ac.uk/archive/projects/reports/peertut4_mary.doc. Accessed 25 September 2007.

Doyle, C. and Robson, K. (2002). *Accessible Curricula: Good practice for all*. Cardiff: UWIC Press.

Earwaker, J. (1992) *Helping and Supporting Students*. Oxford: SRHE/Oxford University Press.

Engineering and Physical Science Research Council (1997) *Research Student and Supervisor: An approach to good supervisory practice.* Swindon: Engineering and Physical Science Research Council.

Entwistle, N. J. and Ramsden, P. (1983). *Understanding Student Learning.* London: Croom Helm.

Evans, P. and Varma, V. P. (1990). *Special Education.* London: Falmer.

Exley, K. and O'Malley, C. (1999). 'Supervising Ph.Ds in science and engineering'. In G. Wisker and N. Sutcliffe (eds), *Good Practice in Postgraduate Supervision*, SEDA Paper 106 (pp. 39–56). Birmingham: SEDA.

Felix, U. (1993). 'Support strategies for international postgraduate students'. *HERDSA News*, 15: 6–8.

Flavell, J. H. (1977). *Cognitive Development.* Englewood Cliffs, NJ: Prentice-Hall.

—— (1979). 'Metacognition and cognitive monitoring: a new area of cognitive developmental inquiry'. *American Psychologist*, 34: 906–11.

Fry, H. and Kettering, J. (eds) (1999). *A Handbook for Teaching & Learning in HE.* London: Kogan Page.

Gibbs, G. (1981). *Teaching Students to Learn.* Buckingham: Open University Press.

—— , Wisker, G. and Bochner, B. (1999). *Supporting More Students.* Oxford: Oxford Brookes University.

Gordon, William J. J. (1961). *Synectics: The development of creative capacity.* New York: Harper.

Grant, A. (2002). 'Identifying students' concerns: taking a whole institutional approach'. In N. Stanley and J. Manthorpe (eds) *Students' Mental Health Needs.* London: Jessica Kingsley.

Gulam, W. A. and Zulfiqar, M. (1998). 'Mentoring: Dr. Plum's elixir and the alchemist's stone'. *Mentoring & Tutoring*, 5 (3): 39–45.

Hall, J. (2003). *Mentoring and Young People: A literature review.* SCRE Research Report 114. Available from www.scre.ac.uk/resreport/pdf/114.pdf. Accessed 25 September 2007.

Hartley, J. and Fox, C. (2004). 'Assessing the mock viva: the experience of British doctoral students'. *Studies in Higher Education*, 29 (6): 727–38.

Hildreth, P., Kimble, C. and Wright, P. (2001). *Computer Mediated Communications and International Communities of Practice.* Conference proceedings of the 1998 Ethicomp. Rotterdam: Erasmus University.

Hodge, B. (1995). 'Monstrous knowledge: doing Ph.Ds in the new humanities'. *Australian Universities' Review*, 38 (2): 35–9.

Holbrook, A. (2002). 'How examiners of doctoral theses utilise the written report'. Paper no. 2, presented at AERA symposium 'Examining the quality of doctoral research'. New Orleans, USA, 1–5 April.

—— and Bourke, S. (2002a). 'Links between research and schools: the role of postgraduate students'. *Australian Educational Researcher*, 28 (2): 15–32.

—— and —— (2002b). 'Ph.D. assessment: design of the study, qualities of examiner reports and candidature information'. Paper presented at AERA Conference New Orleans, 1–5 April.

Honey, P. and Mumford, A. (1986). *Using your Manual of Learning Styles*. Maidenhead: Peter Honey Publications.

Hughes, S. and Wisker, G. (1998). 'Improving the teaching and learning experiences of overseas students'. In C. Rust (ed.) *Improving Student Learning: Curriculum development*. Oxford: Oxford Brookes University.

Jaques, D. (1989). *Personal Tutoring*. Oxford: OCSD.

Johnston, S. (1997). 'Examining the examiners: an analysis of examiners' report on doctoral thesis'. *Studies in Higher Education, Journal of Higher Education*, 22 (3): 333–47.

Kent, M. (2002). 'Online mentoring – a role in widening participation?'. *Learning and Teaching in Action*, issue 1. Centre for Learning and Teaching, Manchester Metropolitan University. Available from www.celt.mmu.ac.uk/ltia/issue1/kent.shtml. Accessed 25 September 2007.

Kiley, M. and Mullins, G. (2002). '"It's a Ph.D., not a Nobel Prize": how experienced examiners assess research theses'. *Studies in Higher Education*, 27 (4): 369–86.

Knight, P. and Yorke, M. (2003). *Learning, Curriculum and Employability*. London: RoutledgeFalmer.

Kolb, D. A. (1984). *Experiential Learning: Experience as the source of learning and development*. Englewood Cliffs, NJ: Prentice-Hall.

Lave, J. and Wenger, E. (1999). 'Legitimate peripheral participation in communities of practice'. In R. McCormack and C. Poechter (eds) *Learning and Knowledge*, (pp. 21–35). London: Paul Chapman Publishing.

Longley, R. and Wald, M. (undated). 'Supporting students with mental health difficulties'. Southern Higher Education Consortium (SHEC) Discussion Paper 7. Available from www.soton.ac.uk/~shec/mentalhealth.htm. Accessed 1 May 2006.

McNamara, D. (ed.) (1997). *Overseas Students in Higher Education*. London: Routledge.

Mahon, D. (2007). 'An investigation into the current nature of one-to-one provision of academic skills in UK Higher Education institutions'. Brunel, unpublished Ph.D.

Main, A. (1980). *Encouraging Effective Learning: An approach to study counselling*. Edinburgh: Scottish Academic Press.

Marton, F. and Säljö, R. (1976). 'On qualitative differences in learning. I – Outcome and process'. *British Journal of Educational Psychology*, 46: 4–11.

Maynard, S. (2006). 'Academic coaching'. Available from www.sandymaynard. com/academic.html. Accessed 3 April 2006.

Melamed, L. (1987). 'The role of play in adult learning'. In D. Boud and V. Griffin (eds) *Appreciating Adults Learning: From the learner's perspective*. London: Kogan Page.

Mental Health Foundation (2006). Available at www.mentalhealth.org.uk.

Meyer, J. H. F. and Boulton-Lewis, G. M. (1997). 'Reflections on learning inventory'. Unpublished questionnaire.

—— and Kiley, M. (1998). 'An exploration of Indonesian postgraduate students' conceptions of learning'. *Journal of Further and Higher Education*, 22: 287–98.

Mezirow, J. (1985). 'A critical theory of self-directed learning'. In S. Brookfield (ed.) *Self-Directed Learning: From theory to practice* (*New Directions for Continuing Education* 25). San Francisco, CA: Jossey-Bass.

Miles, M. and Huberman, M. (1994). *Qualitative Data Analysis*. London: Sage.

Mind Tools (2006). 'Mind tools'. Available from www.mindtools.com. Accessed 17 July 2006.

Morris, C. and Lilly, J. (2006). 'Mind-the-gap report: learning, teaching and access to the curriculum'. Available from http://web.apu.ac.uk/uclt/ research/mindthegap/Learning,_Teaching_&_Access_Report.doc.

Murphy, K. L., Mahoney, Sue E., Chen, Chun-Ying, Mendoza-Diaz, Noemi V. and Yang, Xiaobing (2005). 'A constructivist model of mentoring, coaching and facilitating online discussions'. *Distance Education*, 26 (3): 341–66.

Murray, R. (2002). *How to Write a Thesis*. Buckingham: Open University Press.

Nightingale, P. (1984). 'Examination of research theses'. *Higher Education Research and Development Journal*, 3 (2): 137–50.

O'Connor, K. M. and Oates, L. (1999). *Academic Tutoring*. SEDA Special Paper 11. Birmingham: SEDA.

Okorocha, E. (1997) *Supervising International Research Students*. Issues in postgraduate supervision, teaching and management, series no. 1. Edited by P. Cryer. London: *Times Higher Education Supplement*.

Onyx, J. (2001). 'Implementing work-based learning for the first time'. In D. Boud and N. Solomon (eds) *Work-Based Learning: A new higher education?* (pp. 126–40). Buckingham: SRHE/Open University Press.

Page, B. J., Loots, A. and du Toit, D. F. (2005). 'Perspectives on a South African tutor/mentor program: the Stellenbosch University experience'. *Mentoring and Tutoring: Partnership in Learning*, 13 (1): 5–21.

Paisley, P. O. and Mahon, G. H. (2001). 'School counseling for the 21st century: challenges and opportunities'. *Professional School Counseling*, 5 (2): 106–22.

Parsloe, E. (1995). *Coaching, Mentoring and Assessing: A practical guide to developing competence*. London: Kogan Page.

Particle Physics and Astronomy Research Council (1996). 'An approach to good supervisory practice for supervisors and research students'. Swindon: PPARC.

Peelo, M. and Wareham, T. (2002). *Failing Students in Higher Education*. Buckingham: Open University Press.

Philip, K. (1999). *Young People and Mentoring: A literature review for the Joseph Rowntree Foundation*. Aberdeen: University of Aberdeen.

Phillips, D. (1987). 'Ambivalent allies: myths and reality in the Australian–American relationship'. *Australasian Journal of American Studies*, 6 (2): December.

Phillips, E. and Pugh, D. S. (1994). *How to get a Ph.D.: A handbook for students and their supervisors*, 2nd edn. Buckingham: Open University Press.

—— and —— (2000). *How to get a Ph.D.: A handbook for students and their supervisors*, 3rd edn. Buckingham: Open University Press.

Pitkethly, A. and Prosser, M. (1995). 'Examiners' comments on the international context of Ph.D. theses'. In C. McNaught and K. Beattie (eds) *Research into Higher Education: Dilemmas, directions and diversions* (pp. 129–36). Melbourne: HERDSA.

Preece, R. (1994). *Starting Research*. New York: St Martin's Press.

Quality Assurance Agency (2001). 'The framework for Higher Education qualifications in England, Wales and Northern Ireland', January. Available from www.qaa.ac.uk/academicinfrastructure/FHEQ/SCQF/2001/. Accessed 2 November 2007.

Quality Assurance Agency for Higher Education (2004). 'Code of practice for the assurance of academic quality and standards in HE: postgraduate research programmes'. Available from www.qaa.ac.uk/academic infrastructure/CodeOfPractice/default.asp. Accessed 2 November 2007.

Quinn, E. (2004). 'Academic coach's website'. Available at http://erikaquinn. com. Accessed 3 April 2006, no longer available.

Ramsden, P. (1979). 'Student learning and the perception of the academic environment'. *Higher Education*, 8: 411–28.

Rana, R., Smith, E. and Walkling, J. (1999) 'Degrees of disturbance: the new agenda. The impact of increasing levels of psychological disturbance amongst students in Higher Education'. A report from the heads of university counselling services March 1999. Available from www.hucs.org/hucsreport.html. Accessed 2 November 2007.

Roberts, A. (2000). 'Mentoring revisited: a phenomenological reading of the literature'. *Mentoring & Tutoring*, 8 (2): 145–70.

Roberts, G. (2002). 'Final report of Sir Gareth Roberts' review'. Available at www.hm-treasury.gov.uk/roberts.

Roberts, R. and Zelenyanski, C. (2002). 'Degrees of debt'. In N. Stanley and J. Manthorpe (eds) *Students' Mental Health Needs: Problems and responses*. London: Jessica Kingsley.

Robson, C. (1993). *Real World Research*. Oxford: Blackwell.

Royal College of Psychiatrists (2003). *The Mental Health of Students in Higher Education*. London: Royal College of Psychiatrists.

Samuelowicz, K. (1987). 'Learning problems of overseas students: two sides to a story'. *Higher Education Research and Development*, 6 (2): 121–33.

Schmeck, R. R. (1988). *Learning Strategies and Learning Styles*. New York: Plenum Press.

Schön, D. (1983). *The Reflective Practitioner*. San Francisco, CA: Jossey-Bass.

Slaney, K. (1999). 'Models of supervision for enhancing the English language communication skills of post-graduate students'. In G. Wisker and N. Sutcliffe (eds) *Good Practice in Postgraduate Supervision*. SEDA Paper 106. Birmingham: SEDA.

Stanley, N., Mallon, S., Bell, J., Hilton, S. C. and Manthorpe, J. (2007). *Response and Prevention in Student Suicide*. Preston: Department of Social Work, University of Central Lancashire.

—— and Manthorpe, J. (eds) (2002). *Students' Mental Health Needs*. London: Jessica Kingsley.

—— , —— and Bradley, G. (2000). 'Responding effectively to students' mental health needs: project report'. Hull: School of Community and Health Studies, University of Hull.

Studd, S. (2006). 'Skills Active's role in higher education and presentation of the results of Skills Active's major employer training survey', quoted in report on SkillsActive's Higher Education Conference, Leicester, 2006. Available from: www.skillsactive.com/promotionlist/healthpromotion. Accessed 3 April 2006.

Svensson, L. G. (1987). *Higher Education and the State in Swedish History*. Stockholm: Almqvist & Wiksell.

Taylor, S. and Beasley, N. (2004). *A Handbook for Doctoral Supervisors*. Oxford: RoutledgeFalmer.

Technical & Educational Services Ltd (no date). 'Technical & Educational Services Ltd'. Available from www.53books.co.uk/index.html. Accessed 17 July 2006.

Thomas, L. and Hixenbaugh, P. (eds) (2006). *Personal Tutoring in Higher Education*. London: Trentham Books.

Thomas, P. R. and Bain, J. D. (1982). 'Consistency in learning strategies'. *Higher Education*, 11: 249–59.

Todd, L. (1996). 'Supervising overseas students: problem or opportunity'. In D. McNamara and R. Harris (eds) *Quality in Higher Education for Overseas Students*. London: Routledge.

Trafford, V. N. and Leshem, S. (2002). 'Starting at the end to undertake doctoral research: predictable questions as stepping stones'. *Higher Education Review*, 35, 31–49.

—— and —— (2002b) 'Questions in a doctoral viva'. In UK Council for Graduate Education Research Degree Examining Symposium (London).

University of Lancaster (2003). 'Student mental health policy: planning, guidance & training'. Available from www.studentmentalhealth.org.uk. Accessed 1 May 2006.

Wallace, J. (2004). 'Retention, an intended outcome'. Paper prepared for the Peer Assisted Learning Conference at Bournemouth University, January 2004.

—— (2000). 'Supporting and guiding students'. In H. Fry, S. Ketteridge and S. Marshall (eds) *A Handbook for Teaching and Learning in Higher Education: Enhancing academic practice*. London: Kogan Page.

Walliman, N. (2001). *Your Research Project: A step by step guide for the first time researcher*. Thousand Oaks, CA: Sage.

Waterfield, J. and West, B. (2002). *SENDA Compliance in Higher Education: South West Academic Network for Disability Support*. Plymouth: University of Plymouth.

Watkins, D. and Hattie, J. (1981). 'The learning processes of Australian university students: investigations of contextual and personalogical factors'. *British Journal of Educational Psychology*, 51: 384–93.

Wenger, E. (1998). *Communities of Practice*. Cambridge: Cambridge University Press.

—— (2000). 'Communities of practice and social learning systems'. *Sage*, 7 (2): 225–46.

—— and Lave, J. (1991). *Situated Learning*. Cambridge: Cambridge University Press.

Wheeler, S. and Birtle, J. (1993). *Handbook for Personal Tutors*. Buckingham: Open University Press.

Whitmore, J. (1996). *Coaching for Performance*. London: Nicholas Brearly.

Whittaker, M. and Cartwright, A. (1997a). *The Mentoring Manual*. Aldershot: Gower.

—— and —— (1997b). *32 Activities on Coaching and Mentoring*. Aldershot: Gower.

Winter, J. (1995). *Skills for Graduates in the 21st Century*. London: Association of Graduate Recruiters.

Winter, R., Griffiths, M. and Green, K. (2000). 'The "academic" qualities of practice: what are the criteria for a practice-based Ph.D.?'. *Studies in Higher Education*, 25 (1): 25–37.

Wisker, G. (1999). 'Learning conceptions and strategies of postgraduate students (Israeli Ph.D. students) and some steps towards encouraging and enabling their learning'. Paper presented to the 2nd Postgraduate Experience Conference, Quality in Postgraduate Education, Adelaide.

—— (2000). *Good Practice Working with International Students*. SEDA Paper 110. Birmingham: SEDA.

—— (2005). *The Good Supervisor*. Basingstoke: Palgrave Macmillan.

—— and Sutcliffe, N. (eds) (1999). *Good Practice in Postgraduate Supervision*. SEDA Paper 106. Birmingham: SEDA.

Worley, J. and Martin, M. (2005). 'Writing in the dark: bringing students' writing into the light through peer tutoring. A final report on the project: Exploring the potential of peer tutoring in developing student writing'. *HEA English Subject Centre Newsletter*, 9.

Yorke, M. (1998). 'Assessing capability', in J. Stephenson and M. Yorke (eds) *Capability and Quality in Higher Education*. London: Kogan Page.

Youle, C., Hewitt, P., Muston, R. and Read, J. (2000). *Supporting Students with Mental Health Difficulties*. Milton Keynes: Open University.

Zuber-Skerritt, O. (2002). *Supervising Postgraduate Students from Non-English Speaking Backgrounds*. Buckingham: Open University Press.

JOURNALS

International Journal of Evidence Based Coaching and Mentoring: www.brookes.ac.uk/schools/education/ijebcm/home.html.

International Journal of Mentoring and Coaching: www.emccouncil.org/frames/journalframe.htm.

Mentoring and Tutoring: www.tandf.co.uk/journals/titles/13611267.asp.

USEFUL WEBSITES

The Biotechnology and Biological Sciences Research Council (BBSRC): www.bbsrc.ac.uk/. Accessed 2 November 2007.

British Academy: www.britac.ac.uk/. Accessed 2 November 2007.

Bournemouth University. Peer assisted learning: www.peerlearning.ac.uk/uk_research_summary.html.

Depression Alliance: www.depressionalliance.org/. Accessed 2 November 2007.

Engineering and Physical Sciences Research Council (EPSRC): www.epsrc.ac.uk/default.htm. Accessed 2 November 2007.

The 'Gateway on Research Supervision' provides links to websites offering information, advice and support useful for new supervisors and others involved in supervising and training: www.research-supervision.man.ac.uk/.

Government website (follow link to mental health): www.direct.gov.uk/en/DisabledPeople/HealthAndSupport/. Accessed 2 November 2007.

Medical Research Council: www.mrc.ac.uk/index.htm. Accessed 2 November 2007.

Mental Health Foundation: www.mentalhealth.org.uk/. Accessed 2 November 2007.

Mind: www.mind.org.uk/. Accessed 2 November 2007.

The Natural Environment Research Council: www.nerc.ac.uk/. Accessed 2 November 2007.

Online Tutoring Skills (OTiS) Project Website: http://otis.scotcit.ac.uk/. Accessed 2 November 2007.

Open University 'Making your teaching inclusive' section on mental health difficulties: www.open.ac.uk/inclusiveteaching/pages/inclusive-teaching/recognising-barriers-mental-health-difficulties.php. Accessed 2 November 2007.

PAPYRUS (Prevention of Young Suicide): www.papyrus-uk.org/. Accessed 2 November 2007.

Particle Physics and Astronomy Research Council: www.pparc.ac.uk/home_old.asp. Accessed 2 November 2007.

The Royal Society: www.royalsoc.ac.uk/. Accessed 2 November 2007.

Samaritans: www.samaritans.org/. Accessed 2 November 2007.

Skill: National Bureau for Students with Disabilities: www.skill.org.uk/. Accessed 2 November 2007.

Students in Mind: www.studentsinmind.org.uk/. Accessed 2 November 2007.

Student Mental Health Planning Guidance and Training Manual, compiled by S. Ferguson: www.studentmentalhealth.org.uk. Accessed 2 November 2007.

'Teaching More Students' series, Oxford Brookes University, Oxford: www.brookes.ac.uk/services/ocsld/books/teaching_more_students/index.htm l. Accessed 2 November 2007.

Universities Scotland: www.coshep.ac.uk/. Accessed 2 November 2007.

Universities UK: www.universitiesuk.ac.uk/. Accessed 2 November 2007.

Universities UK (no date) *A Concordat on Contract Research Staff Career Management*; www.universitiesuk.ac.uk/activities/RCIdownloads/rciconcordat.pdf. Accessed 2 November 2007.

University of Brighton, Centre for Learning and Teaching: http://staffcentral.brighton.ac.uk/clt. Accessed 2 November 2007.

University of Brighton, Centre for Learning and Teaching section on Personal Tutoring: http://staffcentral.brighton.ac.uk/clt/resources/personal_tutor.htm. Accessed 2 November 2007.

ORGANISATIONS OFFERING COACHING COURSES AND QUALIFICATIONS

Please note: The editors and publishers of this book do not endorse any organisations or courses mentioned here. Addresses are given for information only.

Achievement Specialists: www.achievementspecialists.co.uk/. Accessed 2 November 2007.

Chartered Institute of Personnel and Development: www.cipd.co.uk. Accessed 2 November 2007.

Newcastle College: www.ncl-coll.ac.uk/. Accessed 2 November 2007.

Oxford Brookes University, Westminster Institute of Education: www.brookes.ac.uk/schools/education/. Accessed 2 November 2007.

Oxford School of Coaching and Mentoring: www.oscm.co.uk. Accessed 2 November 2007.

The Coaching Academy: www.the-coaching-academy.com/. Accessed 2 November 2007.

Index

212